Second Edition

Buzkashi

Second Edition

Buzkashi

Game and Power in Afghanistan

G. Whitney Azoy

WAVELAND
PRESS, INC.

Long Grove, Illinois

For information about this book, contact:
    Waveland Press, Inc.
    4180 IL Route 83, Suite 101
    Long Grove, IL 60047-9580
    847/ 634-0081
    info@waveland.com
    www.waveland.com

This book is dedicated to the memory of Habib Palawan—and to Abdul Khaleq Rafiqi, Ahmad Gul, Baaqi Sabz, Gulab Pushtun, Khosh Mohammed, Tosh Mohammed, and the many other buzkashi people who died in defense of their country.

A march of seventeen miles made in 1837 from Kunduz to Kha-nabad through the thick grass *jangal*, often knee deep in water, performed in a keen winter's evening, had prepared us to wel-come rest and shelter wherever found; and as we stretched our-selves on the comfortable warm felts, and sipped our tea, I felt a glow in my heart that cannot be described. A calmness of spirit, a willingness to be satisfied and pleased with everything around me, and a desire that others should be as happy as myself. How often must every worn-out traveler have expressed this; and why is it that no sooner should we be restored to our wonted vigor than this placid temper leaves us and we suffer ourselves to be ruffled and disturbed by every trivial occurrence?

—Lt. John Wood, *Journey to the Source of the River Oxus*, 1841

Contents

Preface

To the First Edition

Last of all, in return for calling thyself my lord, I say to thee, "Go weep."
—Idanthrysus the Scythian, in response to
an ultimatum from Darius the Great King, 519 B.C.

Two conversations bracket my study of buzkashi. Between them lie six years, nine thousand miles, and a mid-thirties switch in careers. Both encounters featured observations volunteered by close friends. Both dealt with Afghanistan and its spectacular indigenous game.

The first occurred in Kabul during the autumn of 1972. I had been in Afghanistan for six months as an officer at the U.S. Embassy. With a choice of seventeen countries for my first Foreign Service post, I had selected this one for its wild and woolly reputation. Afghanistan, so the history books said, was one of the last frontiers; a land of insurrections and ambuscades, warlord khans and Khyber rifles. Diplomatic life in Kabul, however, had hardly confirmed my rip-roaring expectations. During the weekdays I sat at a smooth desk, pushed typewritten papers, and attended committee meetings run according to standard procedure. My occupational contacts with Afghan government bureaucrats were circumscribed by formality and routine. Protocol ruled the after-hours cocktail circuit. It all seemed extraordinarily pat, incongruously so for Afghanistan.

Such, of course, is inevitable in the life of any diplomatic community for sound and functional reasons. Diplomats, in the very nature of their work, attempt the near impossible: the reconciliation of different national interests across cultural lines. Only by such adherence to certain arbitrary conventions—occupational rules of their own internationalized creation—can diplomats develop the basis of interaction necessary for more substantive work.

As a member of that community, I behaved accordingly. We all did. Even so, it seemed to many of us that the Afghans themselves were really extreme in their emphasis on diplomatic propriety. Professionally, they were masters of protocol. Personally, their brand of hospitality far surpassed reciprocal expectations. Whatever happened, I wondered, to all that wildness and woolliness? How, somewhat more analytically, was I to reconcile these appearances of amicable cooperation with the chronically unrestrained political competition of the past? As recently as 1929, the capital city itself had been overrun by an illiterate bandit from the hills. Nine chaotic months had elapsed before a semblance of order could be restored. Now here were Afghan government officials, barely a generation later, with their perfectly turned phrases, their impeccably pressed suits, and their exquisitely skilled diplomatic manners.

Finally, as the Afghans themselves would say, I made a friend: someone who would really tell me what he thought about things. This honesty-oriented connotation of friendship reveals a set of cultural assumptions: that the true nature of any phenomenon is hidden; that everyone typically tells you whatever suits his situational purposes; and that only the true friend will share the truth as he perceives it. And so, emboldened late one afternoon by the Foreign Ministry ginger ale, I popped the undiplomatic question. How was it, I asked my confidant, that the Afghans I knew were invariably so polite, so hospitable, so apparently ready to agree? How was it possible to be that way all the time, especially in historically chaotic Afghanistan?

His answer, however true in its friendship, was even then essentially indirect. Rather than venture a head-on response, he contented himself with the admission that, yes, I might be right: that, yes, there might be something not entirely real in all that protocol; and that, yes, he could recommend one way for me to pursue the issue. "Here," he said with an eyebrow arched across the pinstriped reception, "here we are always shaking hands and calling each other 'Excellency.' If you want to know what we're really like, go to a buzkashi game."

So I did as he suggested, found myself greatly intrigued, resigned from the Foreign Service (in a generalized fit of middle-aged romanticism for which buzkashi became a suitable exotic symbol), began graduate work at Virginia, and finally returned to Afghanistan as a fledgling anthropologist whose primary purpose was to learn what that cryptic suggestion had meant. By that time, my friend had gone elsewhere as part of his own participation in the game of politics. In the months to come, however, other friends were made—Hafiz, Muhibullah, Manon, Jura, Anwar—and my study would have been impossible without their trust. With my fieldwork finished, I came home to America in early 1978. By that time I knew, or thought I knew, what my first friend had meant half a decade earlier. A second conversation confirmed the matter in dramatic context.

This time, once again, I was talking with an Afghan government official. By virtue of a month of travel shared between us in the United States, he too had become a true friend: To an unusual extent we had come in our relationship to tell it like it was. Now at the end of April the moment had come for us to separate: he back to his Kabul bureaucracy, I to my dissertation first draft. We were, in fact, at the final airport when word reached us of the first communist coup in Afghanistan. All we knew as yet were rumors—not, in other words, the reality of events, but rather the impressions of that reality as perceived by other individuals and communicated to us across a worldwide informational bazaar—and the rumors were that the outcome was still by no means settled. Was president Daoud still alive? Who held Kabul? What of the provinces? The U.S. State Department desk officer for Afghanistan in Washington opined that it was "still too early to characterize the situation." (As far as Afghanistan goes, that statement is never wrong!) I asked my friend what he thought would happen. "You ought to know by now," he said. "You have been studying all about it. Now the buzkashi is about to begin."

Preface

TO THE SECOND EDITION

My heroes have always been cowboys,
And they still are, it seems.

> —Sharon Rice, "Mamas Don't Let Your Babies
> Grow Up to Be Cowboys" (as sung by Waylon Jennings)

You've still got those same lonely songs to remind you
Of someone you seemed to be so long ago.

> —Kris Kristofferson, "Breakdown (A Long Way From Home)"

Much has happened since this book first appeared, almost all of it horrific for Afghanistan. The past quarter century devastated this country more than any other on earth. No country in all history has proven more resilient. No people alive today are more worthy of admiration, respect, and support.

Upon first publication in 1982, my book served mixed purposes. On the one hand, as its author intended, it provided an analytical model. This description of *buzkashi* culture gave newcomers, including some extremely brave media representatives, a hold on the political mayhem around them. Sadly but truly, buzkashi has proven itself an apt metaphor for ongoing Afghan political chaos since 1978. And that violent struggle, while subdued at the moment, could begin again at any time with renewed fury.

On the other hand, and quite unintentionally, the book and its model were taken by some as representing the tone of Afghan culture as a whole. Some Afghanophiles were offended or—which is still less comfortable—confounded by the emphasis on aggression, opportunism, and maximization of spoils. Obviously and mercifully, not all aspects of Afghan experience foreground those themes. To deny their existence, however, or to rationalize them in some comfortably abstract format is delusional. And delusion will only invite a continuation of Afghanistan's agony.

Buzkashi (the literal game) is now being played in new places and by new people. When the Pamir Kirghiz—once the most desperate and today the most intact of Afghan refugee groups—were airlifted from a hellish river bank two decades ago and settled in eastern Turkey, buzkashi came with them. The center of Altintepe, their new village north of Lake Van, has an open field where the game is played by young Kirghiz who've never lived in Afghanistan. Likewise, when young American Green Berets arrived in Mazar-i-Sharif last November, they were taken to Dasht-i-Shadian, south of town, and given horses and shown how to play. In return, the commandos showed onlookers how to cheer American style. Spectator attendance quadrupled in a month. And—gasp!—at least one woman, a brave and excellent American reporter of my acquaintance, was memorably on horseback for the New Year's Day competition.

If buzkashi is spreading as a game—with ongoing and probably impossible talk of a U.S. tour—it must otherwise be put back within game boundaries. The figurative buzkashi must be contained. Doing so, as history tells us, will not be easy.

This new edition retains the first five chapters (with some revisions) and adds two more: one of them historical and ethnographic, the other a frankly personal epilogue. The ethnography update (chapter 6) deals mostly with a period not unlike the present in terms of hopes and plans. In 1988—as in 2002—Afghanistan seemed poised to escape its awful cycle of violence. It did not. Things got not better but worse, much worse. Why?

In part because of lazy and ungrateful indifference from a "free world" which, having fought to the last Afghan against cold war enemies, then abandoned his widow and children. We are told that this shame will not be repeated.

In part, however, things got worse because of another form of indifference or, more precisely, a sympathetic obliviousness by some of Afghanistan's most sincere well-wishers. That wishful blindness to harsh realities must not be repeated. Putting buzkashi back within game borders will now require a clearer recognition of how easily its figurative form can run amok.

Castell d'Argelaguer
January 2002

— Acknowledgements —

This book represents ardent involvement as well as scholarly remove, and in that more personal respect I wish first to recall my father and mother whose enthusiasm for life ranks as my most valued inheritance.

My initial field research (1976–78) was funded by a Fulbright-Hays scholarship administered under the aegis of the Afghan-American Education Commission whose former executive director, Dr. Jon Summers, proved both able bureaucrat and good friend. The late Dr. Louis Dupree, irrepressible and irreplaceable, inspired an entire generation of Afghanistan scholarship, this work included. Academic entrepreneur Thomas Gouttierre was always ready in the early days with useful suggestion and encouragement. Sandy Graham, quick study and perceptive observer, became an integral part of my first field experience.

Intellectually, I am indebted to my faculty members and fellow students at the University of Virginia Department of Anthropology. Roy Wagner, Peter Metcalf, and historian Walter Hauser helped with what in retrospect seems a most cumbersome dissertation. I particularly benefited from the attention of Chris Crocker and David Sapir.

The first edition this book was written on the kitchen table of Lorna Prestwich in Oxford. Renato Rosaldo of Stanford University provided incisive and extremely useful criticism. John McGuigan then produced a slim and elegant volume for the University of Pennsylvania Press.

Subsequent research among Afghan refugees in Pakistan was supported directly by two more Fulbright grants (1982 and 1988) and, indirectly, by institutions as diverse as the International Rescue Committee, the Lawrenceville (NJ) School, and the National Geographic Society. Thanks to such sponsorship I have been able to visit Afghanistan and/or Pakistan, notebook in hand and tape recorder at the ready, almost every year for the last quarter century. Among those whose interest on my behalf went beyond the call of duty are Josiah Bunting, Graham Cole, Robert DeVecci, John Dixon, Peter Dodd, Richard Hoagland, Marilyn Johnson, Bruce Lohof, Michael Malinowski, Randall Martin, and Kent Obee. My understanding was furthered by media friends such as Edward Girardet, Peter Jouvenal, and Donatella Lorch. Now a fledgling journalist myself, I thank Mark Woodward and Todd Benoit of the Bangor *Daily News* and Gordon Lutz of Maine Public Broadcasting; their efforts have helped keep me in the game. This second edition of *Buzkashi* stems from the welcome initiative of Tom Curtin at Waveland Press.

Deepest personal appreciation goes to Brad Hanson who keeps putting me up, and to Ana Tuset who keeps putting up with me.

It is, of course, to the people of Afghanistan that I owe my greatest debt of gratitude. Three men deserve special mention. Sardar Mohammed Hafiz Nawabi whose 1976 introduction to the buzkashi world remains my touchstone of credibility, Ambassador Masood Khalili whose poetic roots and political bravery are a model of what it is to be human, and Sayyed Hussein Hashmi who ("God willing," as Afghans say) will now revivify the *nasl* (race) of buzkashi horses in Afghanistan. My Afghan students during the 1980s and 90s— Masood Farivar, Waseel Azizi, Enayatullah Qasimi, Sonan Osmani, Ahmad Farhad, Wais Osmani, Ashraf Haidari, and Khalilullah Qasimi—are now my teachers.

Other men whom I remember with the vividness of loss (and still more whose names I never even knew) welcomed me, instructed me, and let me into their lives. When I left early in 1978, their future seemed fairly predictable. Political regimes might come and go, but culture and society did not appear under the gun of radical change. Then all became turmoil, and a whole way of life faced annihilation. Many of my closest friends died or were driven into exile. More Afghan friends have been made in the interim. No words can express my thanks to them or their compatriots.

As this second edition is sent to press in early 2002, new hope exists. The purpose of this book is to help provide an analytical context for authentic Afghan recovery. My analysis may seem harsh. This book should be understood against the background of my great love, respect, and admiration for Afghanistan and its people. For what it's worth, I'm with you.

Afghanistan zindabad!

1

THE LAUGHABLE GAME

The rapidity with which the goat sometimes changes masters is very laughable; but the poor animal is occasionally torn to pieces in the scuffle.

—Sir Alexander Burnes, *Cabool*, 1834

Under a cold winter sky the landscape of northern Afghanistan stretches towards a bleak horizon. Here on one rim of the Central Asian steppes, the hard ground runs—gray, yellow, and brown—in an empty latitudinal band below the Hindu Kush. It is less country-side than wasteland: flat with only an occasional low rise, and, even at this time of year, bone dry more often than not. A number of rivers tumble ambitiously northwards from the mountains, but most falter well short of the Russian frontier. Wherever water flows, generations of men have dug fragile irrigation networks, marked now by groves of leafless trees and rows of frozen earth. But these delicate canal patterns, however elaborate in construction and vital for livelihood, exist as exceptions that prove a starkly arid rule: For the farmers and herders who live here, water and well-watered land are critically scarce resources. Beyond a last outlying mud hut, the featureless steppes begin again, desolate and only somewhat less dusty on account of a recent cold rain. And not far from the village, on marginal ground, hundreds of horsemen gather over the mutilated carcass of a calf.

The dead calf is hard for an outsider to see. Unless the earth is still really moist, great clouds of dust hide much of the central action. Powerful men on powerful horses mass with one another in a mayhem of frantic movement: pushing and shoving and changing position and trying to grasp the carcass, headless and hoofless, from

1

the ground. The men are now yelling past one another at the top of their lungs and now urging their horses onwards with an incongruously soft hiss. The horses respond: lurching and rearing, sometimes kicking and biting, and forcing their way towards the center where the carcass lies. Only the best horses and men ever penetrate that far, and only the very best dominate the center for more than an instant: Tosh Palawan, for instance, on the famous *kashka* of Sardar Hafiz, or old Habib on the great roan stallion of Hajji Gulistan. Such horses and, by extension, their riders are said to be able to "stand over the calf until sunset if they feel like it" and so, indeed, to "control the buzkashi."

For most competitors, however, the chance is momentary. In the midst of dust and noise and sweat, the calf comes underfoot. The horse, if well trained, feels the bulk below, braces for an instant, and drops its near shoulder. Clenching his whip between his teeth and cocking one foot behind the saddle, the rider leans and stretches an arm towards the ground. Metal stirrups graze his head, and unshod

TRADITIONAL BUZKASHI. This buzkashi took place in Kizilayaq, Jowzijan province in December 1976, with hundreds of riders. Lunging into the melee from the right is the fabled *kashka* (so-called for its markings) horse of Sardar Hafiz, ridden by the great chapandaz Tosh.

hooves batter his fingers. Lunging half blind in the melee, he manages to grab hold of the carcass briefly, but, as another saying goes, "Every calf has four legs," and other riders quickly wrench it away. Nothing stands still. The calf is trampled, dragged, tugged, lifted, and lost again as one competitor after another tries to gain sole control. Eventually, one horse and rider take the carcass free and clear and let it fall in uncontested triumph. Their victory, however, results in no more than a momentary pause. Already a new play cycle is underway: the increasingly mangled calf carcass on the ground and the mass of horsemen gathering around it.

Hour after hour the wild scene shifts back and forth across an unbounded field. There are winners and losers. Some men never win; no man wins for long. What makes the difference between success and failure? Fate, they say, is always a crucial factor. It would be foolish, indeed vaguely sacrilegious, to argue otherwise. In the world of a buzkashi game, however, a world both volatile and violent, one acknowledges luck but puts his trust in that other ingredient: power.

This book is about buzkashi, not only as a traditional folk game in the form described above, but also as a contemporary sport transformed by the Afghan government. More specifically, it deals with buzkashi in terms of social significance and asks two questions: With respect to Afghan society at various levels of organization, what does buzkashi mean and what does buzkashi do?

Such a here-and-now orientation does not include forays into ethno-history. Suffice it to say that the game began with the Turkic-Mongol peoples who have come from further north and east in a centuries-long series of migrations that ended—if, indeed, it has now really ended—only in the 1930s. Today buzkashi is indigenously shared by several Central Asian ethnic groups resident in northern Afghanistan: not only Uzbeks and Turkmans with whom buzkashi is primarily associated, but also Hazaras, Kazakhs, and even a tiny population of Kirghiz who, unlike most of their brethren now relocated in Turkey, survived the chaotic past quarter century in their remote Pamir valleys by the Chinese border. Other buzkashi participants include Persian speaking Tajiks as well as Pushtun immigrants from south of the Hindu Kush.

Though most of these people (excluding the Pamir Kirghiz) now practice mixed agriculture, they share the equestrian traditions of nomadism. From Scythian times until recent decades, theirs was a world on horseback, and buzkashi remains as a legacy of that bygone era. Understanding its social significance first requires a fuller description of buzkashi—game and sport—which follows immediately. For now, however, there are three ways in which buzkashi relates to society beyond the obvious level of recreational fun:

1. as a commemoration of cultural heritage;
2. as a metaphor for chaotic, uninhibited, and uncontrollable competition; and
3. as an arena in which certain aspects of political competition can actually occur.

Note the incongruity implicit in number three. Nonserious play and serious politics are normally understood as separate and mutually exclusive domains. RFK Stadium and the White House may both be in Washington, D.C., but they house different activities and, except for reciprocal celebrity appearances, serve different purposes.

Life in Afghanistan is less compartmentalized, in part because of a political culture in which power depends ultimately on reputation and the investiture of authority is chronically insecure. With few formal political institutions and legitimacy always at issue, power relationships are constantly in flux. And, as a consequence, all aspects of public experience have political messages, sometimes clear and sometimes implicit. And sometimes-implicit messages—like subliminal advertisements—are all the more effective because those who absorb them are not consciously aware of it. Such is the case even with—indeed, especially with—buzkashi, an ancient game in which participants continue to find new meaning.

This book aims to make such implications clear. Chapter 2 outlines the role of "name" in an unruly political environment. Chapters 3 and 4 describe buzkashi in a series of contexts: local, provincial, and national. Chapter 5 relates buzkashi to the welter of violent events that were occurring when this book first appeared in the early 1980s. Chapter 6 updates that enduring relationship: both phase by phase over the past twenty years and in a detailed account of Afghan refugee buzkashi. The epilogue, while the story of one man, symbolizes by extension the tragedy and courage of a magnificent people. First, however, buzkashi itself.

Buzkashi: Game and Sport

The term *buzkashi* (as used in the Persian *lingua franca* of northern Afghanistan and Kabul) means "goat-grabbing" or "goat-dragging." Among themselves, Turkic speakers sometimes call the game *oghlaq* (young goat). The past century, however, has witnessed a shift in carcass preference. Cattle have become more numerous in the North, and informants maintain that calf bodies better resist dismemberment. Even so, the word *buz* (Persian for goat) is still used in buzkashi to denote the animal carcass of whatever species.

There are two main genres of buzkashi in Afghanistan today. One, commonly called *tudabarai*, is best translated as "emerging from a mass" and thus represents the traditional game form described earlier. The other, known as *qarajai*, takes its name from the "black place" or sense of spatial demarcation that characterizes the newer sport form.

Like so much else in Afghanistan, buzkashi is (and presumably always has been) in flux. These two basic buzkashi types encompass minor regional varieties. All, however, share the same essential components: carcass, horses, and riders. Indeed, the very same individuals, both horses and riders, typically dominate in both main forms. Both forms, furthermore, have the same general objective: gaining control of the carcass and carrying it across space until a score is accomplished.

Otherwise the two forms are considerably different. With regard to objective, the game (tudabarai) is simple and the sport (qarajai) is complex. In tudabarai, the aim is to carry the calf free and clear from everyone else in whatever direction before letting it fall uncontested to the ground. In qarajai, players seek to carry the calf around a standard (generally a flag) and to return it to a scoring circle (close to where play started), at which point the calf is dropped. The various possible directions in which a calf may be carried towards a score are represented in figures 1-1 and 1-2.

If the play objective in tudabarai is simple both to conceptualize and to pursue, its adjudication is quite the reverse. Hence a special potential for quarrel: with no spatial demarcations on the ground, how free is free and how clear is clear? It is precisely over this issue that most of the disputes—disputes that are inherently political as well as merely playful—occur in the traditional form of buzkashi.

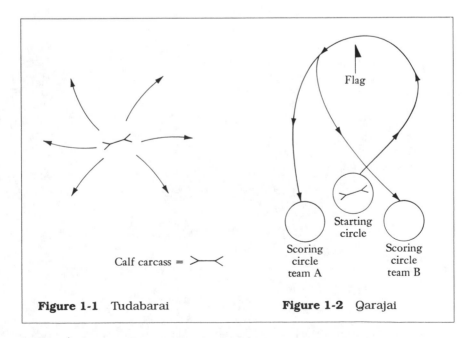

Calf carcass = >—<

Flag

Starting circle

Scoring circle team A

Scoring circle team B

Figure 1-1 Tudabarai   **Figure 1-2** Qarajai

TUDABARAI BUZKASHI. Chapandazan in fur-trimmed caps struggle with each other (and everyone else) in the traditional game. The calf carcass remains invisible on the ground.

QARAJAI BUZKASHI. Only chapandazan may compete in the government sport form, and quickness is more important than brute power. Note the demarcation of space (scoring circle and sideline).

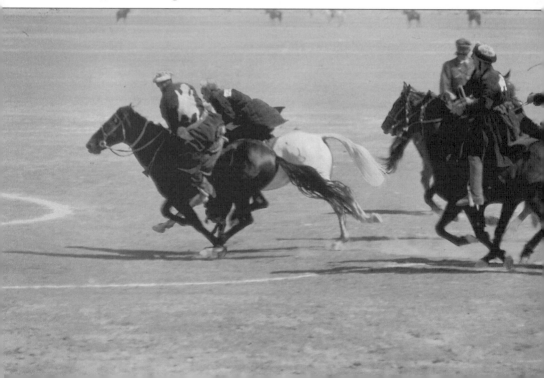

Qarajai, conversely, is more complex in objective but simpler in adjudication. The calf must first be carried around the flag before being dropped in one of the two scoring circles. It is not necessary for the same team to accomplish both objectives in the same play cycle: team A can carry the calf around the flag and team B can drop it in its scoring circle. At the end of a tudabarai cycle, play is resumed wherever the calf was last dropped. In qarajai, on the other hand, the calf is returned to the starting circle at the end of every play sequence.

Two other distinctions of form separate tudabarai and qarajai. First, they are scored differently. In tudabarai, each play sequence is a competitive entity unto itself. Individual scores result in individual rewards—both material and reputational—which are conferred immediately. They have no numerical value, and there is no institutionalized total score at the end of the day. In qarajai, however, the scores are systematically numerical: one point for carrying the calf around the flag; two points for dropping it in the scoring circle. Points are cumulative, and high score wins.

Second, the competitors are organized differently. In tudabarai, it is theoretically every man for himself, with no institutionalization of team identities. Any number of players may participate, and it is not unknown for more than a thousand horsemen to gather at a single game. (Buzkashi people, like humans everywhere, are not strangers to exaggeration. Words like "hundreds" and "thousands" are employed with considerable abandon. But I myself have ridden, timidly and inexpertly, in a tudabarai game with at least 700 riders on the field.) In qarajai, conversely, the players are divided into teams, of which there are ordinarily only two. Here again the equal teams may have any number of players, but the conventional size is somewhere between five and fifteen. The last national championship tournaments in Kabul (late 1970s, early 1980s) featured teams of ten players apiece.

Finally, the two forms of buzkashi correlate, almost without exception, with two sorts of celebratory contexts. The traditional tudabarai game is played under the private sponsorship of an individual and occurs most commonly as part of a *tooi*, or rite of passage. As such, tudabarai is sometimes also termed *qaumi* or, in this sense, "tribal." The emergent qarajai sport is played under public sponsorship and most commonly occurs in keeping with a government-organized holiday festival: calendric, religious, or patriotic. Thus, qarajai is sometimes likewise termed *rasmi* or "official."

PLAY, PARADOX, AND POSSIBILITY

Whether game or sport, buzkashi exists first of all as a form of play. At first inquiry, most Afghans maintain that buzkashi amounts to nothing other than recreation. If the Alexander Burnes term "laughable" misses the strenuously competitive quality of buzkashi (and typifies instead the superciliousness of early European travelers), there can be no doubt that participants involve themselves on the most basic level for the sheer fun of it. Like all play forms, buzkashi constitutes a world apart into which its followers throw themselves with complete abandon. Here is Habib, who still played well into his sxities and who returns at the end of this book:

> Once it starts, nothing else matters. Even beforehand I think about nothing else. Once there was a big buzkashi in Burqa. When I got there, they were already playing. I had a new watch, the one Rashid Khan had given me for riding his horse the week before. I was so excited about this buzkashi that I handed my watch to the first man I met and told him to take care of it. He was a stranger to me, but I was in a hurry. They were already playing. I got right in the game. Afterwards I looked for the stranger, but he was gone. So was the watch, but it was a good buzkashi.

It is, paradoxically, this sense of perceived separateness from the serious stuff of day-to-day reality that enables buzkashi both to be played at all, and to provide thereby an arena for implicitly political events. But for this special perception of play and fun, buzkashi would amount instead to plain combat.

Here participants speak of *shouq*, by which is meant an idiosyncratic interest that particular individuals have in certain leisure activities.[1] There are numerous kinds of shouq pastimes in northern Afghanistan: music, hunting, gambling, wrestling, animal fighting (bird, ram, dog, camel), and buzkashi. Individuals pursue these voluntarily and on a spare-time basis. Thus buzkashi is often described, indeed almost dismissed, in hobby terms as shouq, and this assessment has its own level of truth. Some individuals, admittedly, are more interested than others. Similarly, even the most ardent aficionados have other, more mundane priorities.

Two observations, however, need to be made about the often voiced, in fact normative, notion that buzkashi is "only shouq." The first has to do with precisely what type of individual is at the core of buzkashi. The second is concerned with how the concept of shouq facilitates the enacting of politically meaningful events in an arena which otherwise could not exist.

Countless males from all segments of society in northern Afghanistan share interest in the game. Powerful and weak, rich and poor, old and young—each of these categories includes individuals for whom buzkashi is a shouq. All such interested persons are here analytically encompassed by the term "participants," in that all are involved in the buzkashi experience. Such participation, however, can assume many forms that at a minimum include competitor, spectator, and sponsor. Of these, the status of sponsor is always primary. In all its various forms and contexts, buzkashi depends upon individuals who undertake to sponsor horses, riders, and, most importantly, entire occasions on which it is played.

Sponsorship identity is the first factor that elevates the game's social significance above the level of mere shouq: These sponsors are almost without exception the very individuals, the *khans*, who otherwise dominate politics beyond the bounds of buzkashi. In this regard, the game exists very much as an elitist institution. Only the powerful and rich can hope to muster the considerable resources, both political and economic, necessary to sponsor a buzkashi.

A second qualification to the "only shouq" dismissal springs from the first. The khans—all members of an amorphous and individually hyperambitious political elite—are invariably in competition with one another. This constant rivalry, despite the fact that everyone accepts it as normal, goes against Islam-based ideals of cooperation. Khans seldom show their enmity in open, public discourse. Indeed, the state of their rivalries—who's with whom and against whom and with what effect—is mostly disguised. Buzkashi, by virtue of being "only a game" which "doesn't count," provides a *sanctioned* arena in which this process can occur publicly and be observed by one and all. Herein lies the subtle, crucial paradox: Khans support buzkashi "for the fun of it," but their play competition inevitably assumes extra-play overtones.

All games are inherently ambiguous. Are they "for fun" or "for real"? With buzkashi, a violent form of physical competition all too similar to equestrian battle, this ambiguity can be especially pronounced, especially among participants who are real-life antagonists. Gregory Bateson describes the subtlety involved: "Play could only occur if the participant organisms were capable of some degree of metacommunication, i.e., of exchanging signals which carry the message 'this is play.'"

And again: "The statement 'this is play' looks something like this: 'These actions in which we now engage do not denote what those actions *for which they stand* would denote.'"[2] Buzkashi experience, far more so than that of any other shouq, is characterized by only the finest of lines between nonserious play and nonplayful seriousness. Real-life grudges are readily activated in the thick of a buzkashi melee, and outright fighting can result. Even more disruptive to the play ethos (and thus to the entire celebratory occasion) are the struggles for authority that inevitably arise throughout the buzkashi process. Despite all attempts to preserve the festival atmosphere of good-fellowship, the same question is foregrounded time and again: Who is in control here? What begins as idiosyncratic shouq can quickly become public politics.

For reasons elaborated in chapter 2, members of the khan elite—and, indeed, all individuals in this society whose relationships shift from situation to situation—are most reluctant to risk political show-downs in public where impressions of weakness would be too vividly observable. On account of its normative loophole that "this is only shouq," buzkashi affords an exception to that pattern of behavior. On the one hand, it provides an arena wherein individuals can compete for authority and thereby, in a cyclical process, the reputation for authoritativeness. Winners in this competition have their "names" enhanced. On the other hand, it is "only play" in the sense that losers can lick their wounds with some external display of indifference.

As the sequence of buzkashi events proceeds across time, whether for an afternoon or for several days, their participants shift, in the formulation of Erving Goffman,[3] back and forth between the twin "frames" of play and seriousness: now the one, now the other, now somewhere in the indeterminate middle ground. Thus the play element exists as background to this study, and its ambiguity must always be borne in mind.

Finally, the sheer numbers of persons who participate in buz-kashi far exceed those associated with other shouqs. Whether on the scale of locality, province, or nation, buzkashi play attracts thou-sands, even tens of thousands, of participants. No other event (save for the prayers held at certain mosques on Moslem festival days) gathers so many people together in traditional society. Even on the national level in Kabul, the attraction of buzkashi compares favor-ably with that of other celebratory events. In an analysis such as this one, where Durkheimian assumptions of social solidarity are quali-fied by an emphasis on individuals, it is somewhat contradictory to argue in terms of collective representations. To the extent, however, that such phenomena exist in socially atomized Afghanistan, buz-kashi can claim near-universal appeal.

COMMEMORATION, METAPHOR, AND ARENA

As stated earlier, there are three dimensions to the social signifi-cance of buzkashi in Afghanistan: (1) as a commemoration of cultural heritage, (2) as a metaphor for unbridled competition, and (3) as an arena for political process. This book is primarily concerned with the third of these dimensions; with the ways in which the play situations of buzkashi are imbued, however subtly, with issues of authority and power. The first two dimensions, however, deserve some preliminary elaboration, both as items of buzkashi interest in their own right and as factors that contribute to its symbolic power in the political realm.

COMMEMORATION OF CULTURAL HERITAGE

The horsemen themselves answer the question of buzkashi origins succinctly. "It comes," they are fond of saying, "from our fathers and grandfathers." For Northerners and now increasingly for other Afghans as well, buzkashi possesses a special significance. In no other form of sanctioned activity are the cultural values of masculinity—courage, strength, dominance, host generosity—so vividly embodied. As such, buzkashi still serves as the centerpiece for traditional rite-of-passage celebrations in the North. On these occasions of circumcision or (more rarely) marriage, a wide range of activities is combined into one interrelated experience that provides continuity across generations. The actual rite of passage, however, occurs in domestic seclusion. The great numbers of guests have been invited for the buzkashi.

Somewhat more specifically, buzkashi also commemorates a particular aspect of the past: equestrian culture and the long-ago grandeur associated with it by present-day Turkic-Mongol descendants. In the guesthouse of his compound on the edge of the steppes west of Kunduz, Abdul Ali, who in his prime as an Uzbek buzkashi rider had "a name known by all the men in their fields and all the women in their houses," recalls the much earlier heyday of his ethnic nationality:

> Once we had the power. It was our turn then, and from the time of Timur (Tamurlain) no one could stop us. No one else had so many horses. No one else could ride them so well. We had it all. It was our turn then, but now the turn has passed. It's the turn of the Pushtuns now. They have the power. The turn has passed. Land, money, prestige—it's all in their hands now.

Earlier still, it was in the general region of Central Asia that the horse was first domesticated, and geographers of antiquity such as Herodotus and Hsuan Tsang remark on its central importance. Though used also as a source of food, clothing, and shelter, the horse was primarily employed in two critical activities of nomadic life: herding and raiding. This dependence lasted into the nineteenth century:

> . . . they breed sheep, camels, and horses: and so numerous is the latter, that there is scarcely a man in Toorkestan so indigent as to walk on foot: even beggars travel on horseback, or at least upon camels and asses. As might be expected in such a people, the Uzbeks produce swarms of light cavalry and are renowned for their exertions in predatory war."[4]

Not surprisingly for an item of such fundamental utility, the horse appears in artistic expressions of nomadic culture. The earliest pile-weave carpet as yet unearthed, 2400 years old, displays an equine border. Because accumulation of material items was incompatible with mobility, most creativity tended towards verbal forms, and in Turkic sagas the horse figures to particularly good effect: saving the day when all seems lost, and never (in sharp and positive contrast to most human characters) wavering in its loyalty.[5] In the seventeenth-century folk epic of Kurroglou (well known to Abdul Ali), the hero is only as good as his horse Kyrat, who warns of an enemy approach, leaps a chasm in the nick of time, and aids in the escape of a princess.

The successes and failures of Kurroglou correlate exactly with the presence and absence of his wonder horse. In his last words he addresses the men who are about to murder him, "You have killed my Kyrat, there is my bosom, strike, without him I am useless in this world."[6]

In traditional steppe culture, the finest horses were kept by the most powerful individuals for purposes of status display. By the mid-nineteenth century this practice had extended southwards to Kabul, where Dost Mohammed, the Pushtun *amir*, maintained a prize stable.

> In the spring he viewed his stud daily about three or four P.M. He sat on a terrace made for the purpose, two or three feet high, covered with felts. Here many of his chiefs joined him who did not usually attend the morning durbar. These were stipendiary lords, and moolahs or priests and familiar friends who enjoyed his confidence; they passed their time in smoking the cullion, desultory conversation, complimentary commendations of the prince's fancy for horses, and admiration of the promising brood of young colts, which were the delight of his highness and favorites of his taste.[7]

With the decline of nomadism, the horse no longer exists so much as an ecological essential, but it has kept its status value to a remarkable extent. Powerful khans in the rural North still buy and breed the best horses and go in factional delegations to neighboring provinces in the hope of obtaining even finer animals. Champion stallions are ostentatiously tethered in the residential compound, and the "complimentary commendations" remain as obligatory as in Kabul a century ago.[8] Even when more contemporary forms of transport are available, khans ride their favorite horses to certain traditional occasions such as a council of local leaders, a nearby funeral, or a tooi. Finally, it is in buzkashi play that the reputation of a khan is most directly associated with the prowess of his horse.

As a traditional game in northern Afghanistan, the equestrian experience of buzkashi embodies strong elements of indigenous cultural heritage, a whole range of meanings associated with the heroic man-on-horseback era. As an emerging sport in provincial centers and in Kabul, it is coming to be accepted as an institution whose

THE KASHKA OF SARDAR MOHAMMED HAFIZ NAWABI. Blanketed and receiving its groom's full attention, this was the most famous horse in all ▶ 1970s Afghanistan.

meanings are relevant to the shared heritage of an entire country. Whatever transpires in the course of a buzkashi is thus imbued with special importance. On account of its links with the past, buzkashi in the present is symbolically larger than life.

BUZKASHI AS A METAPHOR FOR UNBRIDLED COMPETITION

"If you want to know what we're really like, go to a buzkashi game." The suggestion that inaugurated this study implied, at least to me at that time, some sort of mystification: that underneath all cooperative appearances of protocol there lay quite another ethic, more fundamentally true. I, of course, was the only one mystified. No Afghan really believes that the social ambience in which he lives is all a matter of "shaking each others' hands and calling each other 'Excellency.'" Too much of day-to-day existence is too stridently contentious for such naiveté to thrive. On the other hand, the statement of my friend as it stands is incomplete, for in order to be provocative, he oversimplified: self-evidently, it is only *sometimes*—only occasionally, perhaps, but then spectacularly—that life is "like a buzkashi."

As a whole, social experience in this society is much the same as anywhere else: a complex process characterized by both cooperation and competition. The "go to a buzkashi game" suggestion might better have been prefaced, "If you want to know what we're really like sometimes but almost never admit to openly." Here is the second dimension of social significance to buzkashi: it acts as a metaphor for the particular sort of unbridled competition—chaotic, uninhibited, and uncontrollable—that lurks below the apparently cooperative surface.

The notion that games possess this singular capacity for enunciating otherwise unacknowledged principles of experience is not new. Clifford Geertz, in particular, makes much the same point:

> Balinese go to cockfights to find out what a man, usually composed, aloof, and almost obsessively self-absorbed, a kind of moral autocosm, feels like when attacked, tormented . . . he has totally triumphed or totally been brought low.[9]

In buzkashi, however, the revelation is less psychological than sociological: it is not an individual, but an aggregation of individuals who behave with so untypical a lack of restraint. Social life can abruptly shift from the orderly to the chaotic on any level of interaction. The buzkashi comparison describes events that range from knock-down-drag-out fights among children to serious pushing and shoving in front of a bakery shop to intrafamily inheritance conflicts that get out of hand (and, worst of all, become common knowledge). With the coup of April, 1978, the largest buzkashi of all began: handshakes became clenched fists, and Their Excellencies were executed.

No other ceremonial events dramatize this side of experience so vividly. None of the various animal fights that so delight their fans involve human combatants. Traditional wrestling matches between men are narrowly stylized and lack inherent potential for explosion. The other main public spectacles are either religious or patriotic: the end of Ramazan, for instance, or Independence Day. These latter two genres of events may, on occasion, evoke adversarial emotions towards outsiders, but within the community of celebrants all is fellowship. Both genres, furthermore, are nonproblematic: participants know at the start what will happen and how it will end.

Little wonder, then, that the Habibs of Afghanistan "think about nothing else" when a buzkashi begins. First, the game expresses not only the orderly and cooperative facet of experience—getting together for a good time—but also its competitive, in fact its uncontrollably competitive, counterpart: the not generally acknowledged but unmistakably real associability that simmers beneath an all-too-brittle surface. Second, its problematic character makes the game and what the game signifies all the more engrossing. Much public ceremony is blandly predictable, and eyelids droop surreptitiously at prayers or parades. At a buzkashi no one knows who will score next or fall flat. Indeed, the problematic quality of this particular game can extend well beyond the calf carcass struggle and into politics.

BUZKASHI AS AN ARENA FOR POLITICAL PROCESS

So far this discussion has dealt with socially expressive aspects of buzkashi: as a commemoration of cultural heritage and as a metaphor for unbridled competition. Both of these are important. Both hold interest for insider buzkashi participants and outsider observers of culture. Together these meanings account for the remarkable capacity of buzkashi to attract participants and to concentrate their attention; to render, in other words, the experience of buzkashi symbolically powerful with an intensity beyond that of mundane life. This intensity is then transmitted into a third—and far more remarkable—dimension of social significance.

F. G. Bailey begins *Stratagems and Spoils* with the words, "Think of politics as a competitive game."[10] For him, politics is a processual struggle with players, prizes, rules, and referees. This study of buzkashi takes Bailey at his word and then reverses the simile. Here we think of a competitive game as politics.

Normatively, of course, such a claim would be discounted by many, perhaps even most, buzkashi participants who say that their only motivation for involvement is shouq. Do they believe what they say? Here is a critical question without a simple answer. Some probably do, particularly those who, for whatever reason, lack political sophistication. For them, a game is a game is a game. At the other extreme, there are clearly some who recognize its symbolic potential and manipulate accordingly. Others, almost certainly the majority, are, in effect, half conscious of buzkashi as an arena in which events have real-life implications of authority and power. For these men, virtually all aspects of public existence are vaguely political, but many of these aspects—buzkashi among them—are ordinarily not objectified as such.

Of all those who disclaim a relationship between buzkashi and politics, the most adamant are the khans—exactly the ones, that is to say, with the most political prominence. They participate as sponsors, so their usual explanations go, either for the fun of it or, with a typically khan-like sense of noblesse oblige, "to give everyone else a good time." Their clients, however, sometimes vouchsafe a very different reaction. Attitudes are generally guarded, but here are the words of one such subordinate, at once the penniless groom of a powerful khan and a good friend of mine, who after several months felt secure enough with me to risk some indignant candor:

> A man gives a large tooi, spends a lot of money, gives a lot of prizes . . . it's all for a name. Now take the *rais* (or government-appointed provincial "president" of buzkashi—see chapter 4): no salary, no wages, but he spent 20,000 Afghanis for a single party (at the Kunduz interprovincial tournament). All for the name. To be called rais sahib, rais sahib, oh rais sahib everywhere he goes. So the President [of Afghanistan] will know him. It's all name. Oh rais sahib. This money he spent on the party: 20,000 afghanis. What's the benefit? You tell me. Give it to the poor and naked; that's different. But no, it's all name. He's the rais sahib, the rais sahib.

The spectacular play quality of buzkashi—its wild fun—makes this more mundane dimension hard to grasp. If confronted with the issue, many Afghans might argue (honestly if superficially) that the principals in buzkashi play are not the khan sponsors at all but rather their client riders, called *chapandaz* (pl. *chapandazan*), who dominate the actual competition for control over the calf carcass. Certainly it is these men, distinct with their fur-trimmed wool helmets from the otherwise turbaned assembly, who monopolize the spatial center of any buzkashi game struggle. One or another of the khans or indeed, anybody else, may occasionally try his own luck in tudabarai where, as the saying goes, "everyone has the right" to reach for the calf, but success is rare. In provincial and national play, moreover, with its qarajai form, only the chapandazan are allowed on the field. The political leaders—khans, governors, heads of state—all sit on the sidelines.

Thus it does appear to some that the principals in these two activities—buzkashi and politics—are not the same and that the domains are indeed separate. Only on account of this normative notion can buzkashi be played. Its importance as a political arena, however, and the centrality of political leaders within it depends on the realization that buzkashi entails, at least analytically, not one but three interrelated orders of competitive game. All three, to remember Bailey, are related to a fourth-order game of real-life politics that exists, for the most part, beyond the boundaries of buzkashi.

Only the first-order game, the actual buzkashi "play" already described, is recognized as such by its participants. All four, however, are competitive and problematic. All four are inherently concerned with control. All four, finally, are "zero-sum," in that prizes are scarce and winners succeed at the expense of losers (even though measures of victory and defeat are typically susceptible to ambiguous interpretation). All four orders of game occur simultaneously, and the essential struggle in each may be summarized as follows:

> *First-order game*—The buzkashi play competition itself, in which participants compete for control of the calf carcass and in the process of which disputes often occur;
>
> *Second-order game*—The competition for control over the first-order game as a whole, and especially over the disputes that arise from the first-order game;
>
> *Third-order game*—The competition for control over the entire celebratory enterprise which the buzkashi represents; and
>
> *Fourth-order game*—The competition for control over the entire real-world political process in which buzkashi participants (and everyone else in the society) are encapsulated.

The crux of this study hinges on the notion that there exists a causal relationship among these four orders of game, that what happens in one can and does have effects on the other three. It is relatively easy to anticipate how such a relationship could exist with the arrows of causation going from higher to lower orders of game: how the power of a khan in mundane politics (fourth-order game) might enable him to afford a premier horse-rider combination capable of controlling the calf (first-order game), or how his real-life authority (again, fourth-order game) could lead to control over buzkashi play disputes (second-order game). Such a dynamic would seem, purist protestations notwithstanding, to characterize institutional play in many societies. Far more remarkable is the reverse process whereby the causation arrows run from lower to higher orders of game; whereby, in other words, what happens in buzkashi has effects on politics.

The bulk of this book deals in various ways with this reverse dynamic. It operates not only on the local level where khans sponsor their toois, but also on the levels of province and nation where government officials perform analogous roles. At this point in the discussion, however, two disclaimers are in order.

The first is obvious. It would be absurd to argue that as buzkashi goes so goes Afghanistan. There is vastly more to politics than this

ancient and picturesque pastime. Political conflicts, whether they have
to do with one furrow of irrigated ground outside some remote village or
with the military airfield at Bagram outside Kabul, are by no stretch of
the imagination determined only by who won the last buzkashi. Rather,
buzkashi is a part—a relatively small part, perhaps, but certainly a vivid
one—of the total political process in which authority depends ultimately
on impressions derived from a wide spectrum of events.

The subtlety involved helps explain, if not necessarily excuse, the
need for a second disclaimer. Documentation of the links among the
various orders of game is somewhat uneven in this study. It is quite
clear among the first three orders (all of which deal with various
aspects of the buzkashi occasion), but, for the most part, only inferen-
tial in the critical links between those first three orders (buzkashi)
and "real-world" politics. In no instance can it be "proven" that a specific buzkashi event solely resulted in a specific political development:
the making or breaking, for instance, of some khan. Here, however,
the weakness of argument only reflects the ambiguous strength of
games whose potential for political effect depends precisely on its non-
objectification. For just that reason, no informant will ever describe an
important political rise or fall as a function of buzkashi alone.

What, then, can be documented, and how best to document it?
The most useful approach is to start with the buzkashi process itself
and to proceed from there, upwards and outwards. This strategy
generates a series of realizations: first, that the locus of authority is a
problem at all phases of buzkashi; second, that this problem is
taken seriously by the buzkashi participants; third, that this seriousness belies the normative notion that the game is only a game; and
fourth, that the entire process serves as an implicit arena for the display of political competence. For if buzkashi, empowered by its cultural past and spectacular in pell-mell present, exists as a metaphor
for uncontrollability, what better public opportunity could there be
for the demonstration of control?

This action, however, makes sense only within its setting. And
thus, before re-entering the game, we must first examine the society
in which it holds such significance: an unruly society where, as in
buzkashi, individual actors struggle for control and gain it—if at
all—only for as long as they can hang on.

NOTES

[1] For a more elaborated discussion of shouq, see Slobin, Mark, *Music in the
Culture of Northern Afghanistan* (Tucson: University of Arizona Press,
1976), pp. 23–24.
[2] Bateson, Gregory, *Steps to an Ecology of Mind* (New York: Ballantine
Books, 1972), pp. 180–181.

[3]Goffman, Erving, *Frame Analysis* (New York: Harper and Row, 1974).

[4]Elphinstone, Montstuart, *An Account of the Kingdom of Caubul* (London: Oxford University Press, 1972 [first published 1815]), vol. II, p. 193.

[5]Chadwick, N. and V. Zhirminski, *Oral Epics of Central Asia* (Cambridge: Cambridge University Press, 1969), p. 15.

[6]Chodzko, A., *Specimens of the Popular Poetry of Persia* (London: Oriental Translation Fund of Great Britain and Ireland, 1828), p. 341.

[7]Harlan, J., *A Memoir of India and Afghanistan* (Philadelphia: J. Dobson, 1842), pp. 150–151.

[8]Each time I visited a different khan for the first time, we would start with a brief inspection of his best horses tethered conspicuously in the courtyard. I would admire (with a woefully untrained eye) this or that marvelous quality, nod with apparent discrimination, and exclaim what a fine horse it was. The khan or his groom would respond with details of pedigree, diet, and recent buzkashi performance.

The association of fine horses with prestige seems to survive social change. One provincial governor with an international background was a newcomer to the North and had no horses of his own. Soon, however, he started to take visitors from Kabul to the rural compound of a favored khan horse owner where the cycle of admiration would take place as if the horses were his. Each time, almost on cue, the khan would go through the motions of offering his best horse to the governor as a gift. It was always graciously refused and remained in readiness for the next visit.

Another fieldwork anecdote recalls the afternoon reveries of Dost Mohammed. I was most fortunate in having as a friend an individual whose horse was universally recognized as among the very best in Afghanistan. Unlike most buzkashi khans, however, he is very much a man of the world, with residences in his northern hamlet, Kabul, and London. A remarkable person, he moves with grace between these disparate locales. Occasionally their conflicting demands get too much for even him. "At times like these," he once confided, "all I really want to do is be in the stable by my horse."

[9]Geertz, Clifford, "The Balinese Cockfight," *Daedalus* 101, 1 (1972): 27.

[10]Bailey, F. G., *Stratagems and Spoils* (Oxford: Basil Blackwell, 1969).

2

REPUTATION AND THE UNRULY AFGHAN

And far from the Sulieman heights comes the sound of the stirring tribes,

Afridi, Hazara, Ghilzai, they clamour for plunder and bribes;

And Herat is held but by a thread; and the Uzbek has raised Badakhshan;

And the chief may sleep sound, in his grave, who would rule the unruly Afghan.

—Sir Alfred Lyall, "The Amir's Soliloquy "

With my diplomatic brand of Kabuli Persian less than wholly serviceable in the hinterland, early fieldwork conversations tended towards the simplistic. Fairly comfortable with concrete talk about buzkashi play, I felt less well equipped to probe the abstractions of its political context. Time and again, some variant of a single dialogue would begin bravely but then stop short or, rather, recycle in what suggested itself as a tautology born of my own linguistic incompetence: "Why," I would ask, "is that man so important?"

"Because," the answer would come, "he has a name (*nam*)."

"What good is a name?"

"It gives a man supporters."

"What good are supporters?"

"They help a man succeed with his 'work.'"

"What happens when his 'work' is successful?"

"It gives a man a name."

So it would go, discouragingly, while I strained ear and tongue for a fuller sense of the language. With time and vernacular competence, various other research issues were gradually elaborated and tentatively resolved. The dynamics of political authority, however, remained a puzzle of apparently deceptive clarity. Surely, I told myself, there must be more to it than the reciprocal process of reputation and followers: some formal institutions, surely, and some readily defined positions within them.

These latter qualities, so familiar to participants in politics of the modern state, simply never appeared: certainly not in traditional society, and not in any fundamental sense (incumbent-sponsored images to the contrary) within national government organization. Instead, my most durable model remained that of the folk hero Kurroglou, whose legend still epitomizes Afghan politics.

His is the saga of the self-made man for whom the momentum of impressions is all-important. Well but not nobly born, Kurroglou falls from favor with the patron of his family, turns the tables, and (thanks to his wonder horse) defeats the old leader. The hero now acquires supporters of his own, who are impressed with such exploits and perceive in them the likelihood of future spoils. Ever greater exploits attract ever more followers, and in the end Kurroglou dies only through treachery. From event to event, the cyclical process continues: reputation leads to supporters, which lead to successes, which lead to spoils, which lead back to reputation.

Now as then, successes and spoils are the aggressively active ingredients in this process. Only by means of successes and spoils, the more publicly demonstrable the better, can a man gain reputation and thus authority over supporters. Such an emphasis on exploits helps explain why this society has never gotten a good press for political organization—why, for instance, after two dozen years of conflict Afghanistan remains beleaguered by viciously self-seeking warlords.

Here the analysis must take heed: ethnography is all too often debilitated by negative terms. With regard to Afghanistan, however, facts must be faced. Sanitized Afghanophile memoirs and travelogues notwithstanding, politics here are inherently bellicose, notoriously "unruly" beyond the standards of most other cultures and countries. The post-1978 chaos, however extraordinary in scale and exacerbated by outsiders, has largely been an expression of fault lines within Afghanistan itself. Only against that volatile background can the dynamic of politics by reputation—and the relevance of buzkashi to that dynamic—be understood.

With authority dependent on reputation and reputation on exploit, unrest is the ancient theme of political life. In 1273, Marco Polo noted of the northern region that "the people have all taken refuge in fortresses among the mountains, on account of the Banditti and armies that harass them."[1] Six hundred years later, two other European travelers found the situation much the same:

> The amount of rivalry and intrigue that exist among the petty khans of Turkestan is perfectly incredible to anyone who has not been in the country; and, instead of trying to decrease or modify either, they exert their intelligence to complicate and carry out their paltry schemes . . . They recognize the suzerainty of the princes of Herat, Bokhara, and Khulm, only because they have not sufficient power to throw it off, or, that occasionally it happens to be in their interest to acknowledge it. They will change their protectors as often as it suits them . . . This continuous struggle of agitation, intrigue, perfidy, and dominion seems to be an innate necessity to a khan; it has existed from earliest times, and will certainly be the same a thousand years hence.[2]

and

> The whole tract of land on this side of the Oxus, as far as the Hindu Kush and Herat, has, from ancient times, been the field of continual quarrels and warfare; and these have involved not only the small predatory states in its vicinity, Kunduz, Khulm, Balkh, Aktche, Seripul, Shibergan, Andkhuy, Bedakhshan, and Maymene, but the emirs themselves, both of Bokhara and Kabul. These princes, to carry out their plan of conquest, have been ever ready to kindle the flames of dissension; sometimes, too, they have taken an active part in these differences.[3]

Thanks essentially to developments in technology and administration, the Kabul-based central government had—until the current disruptions that started in 1978—gradually increased its control over the hinterland in this century, and its bureaucratic network functioned elaborately on the levels of province and subprovince. This elaboration (governors, subgovernors, law courts, police detachments) was, however, really effective only in the immediate towns. Even in the most stable of periods, the government writ has seldom run with consistent force beyond the few paved roads. A truer conception of political life in the countryside is provided by the castle-like architecture of khan compounds with their massive mud walls and great wooden gates. These rural fortresses are never left without at least one adult male inside, and every such household has its own arsenal. The quality of 1970s day-to-day existence was, informants told me, more tranquil than in their grandfathers' day: after all, the most flagrant brigandage of two or three generations ago had been inhibited by the threat of government intervention. Even so, the only reliable hope for security lies, immemorially, in self-help coupled with reputation. Every individual, at most every residential compound, ultimately stands alone with whatever clients or allies or patrons can be mustered for the moment, and "the unruly Afghan" remains the critical unit of political structure.

Thus my fieldwork search for neatly defined institutions of authority ultimately revealed no such thing. For all practical purposes, the Afghan form of authority resides neither in permanent corporations nor in formal statuses, but in individual men who relate to each other in transient patterns of cooperation and competition. Only through some degree of cooperation can land be farmed, canals dug, livestock raised, and women exchanged. Unregulated, however, by any system of universally recognized authority, this cooperation readily gives way to competition. Fragilely constituted groups fragment under the weight of changing circumstances, and every man is left to fend for himself with his ambitions, his wits, his material wealth, his immediate family, and most of all, his reputation.

The burden of this chapter deals with reputation: its development, its maintenance, and its purposes. Some of the perils entailed in its loss are discussed in chapters 3, 4, and 5. First, however, the analysis must briefly digress (and once again run the risk of negativism) in order to answer a critical question: How is it that the political field is so full of persons potentially available as clients for self-styled patrons? How is it that such potential followers are not already bound by membership in some unit of social organization whose authority they recognize in a comprehensive sense?

It is a difficult problem made all the more so by the inconsistencies which plague Afghan observations on the matter. In one breath, informants would express the inviolability of certain social groups; men of the same this or that always hung together no matter what. A sense of benign self-righteousness indicated that here was all I needed to know. The very next remark, however, would often deal with an immediate example of perfidy as someone (seldom, if ever, the speaker himself) shifted sides opportunistically with the reputational flow.

FOUR TIES THAT DO NOT ALWAYS BIND

Afghans interact and find common ground primarily on the basis of four social principles: kinship, residence, class, and religion. All these imply ties that are supposed, rhetorically, to transcend individuality. Much truth exists in this rhetoric, but it is not the whole truth. Normative protestations to the contrary, none of these four principles gives rise to fully binding corporate group organization. None provides a clear framework within which leadership status is unequivocally defined. Ties, while binding in theory, are not infrequently broken—and quite frequently manipulated—by politically ambitious individuals. We take each of the four principles in turn.

The principle of kinship supplies the most significant institutions in the lives of most Afghans. Descent is universally patrilineal with membership organized in a segmentary lineage system. No Afghan would argue with this neat description, and the prospect of any other kinship mode is simply unthinkable. Conflict arises instead over issues of leadership within the descent group and results from a striking weakness in patrilineal organization. Authority is specified no further than the level of residential family. Within such a household, which may include three or even four generations, the locus of authority is clear. Barring some mental disability, the generationally senior male is acknowledged as having legitimate control over all those descended from him except female offspring who have married. It is this patriarch who acquires or alienates land, initiates irrigation, negotiates client contracts, and arranges marriages. His death, however, leaves the family without specified procedures for succession to leadership.

Strict Islamic inheritance rules divide the patrimony into equal shares for sons (and lesser shares for wives and daughters) so that no one heir assumes material supremacy over the others. Without such a basis of disproportionate wealth, no one son can automatically succeed to senior status, and this absence of primogeniture precludes over time the unchallenged development of a preeminent lineage. Brothers, formerly united in obedience to their live father, now find themselves potentially at odds. The post-mortem process of actual inheritance division is particularly stressful, and latent tensions can break into the open with the uncontrollable force of a buzkashi. Even in the most amicable instances, the issue of authority has now become an open question: Which brother, henceforth, will take the lead in fraternal enterprise? Brotherly sentiment usually overcomes whatever tendencies towards rampant competition, but not without inevitable problems. Considerably more ambivalent is the relationship between brothers' sons. The *bacha-i-kaka* can be either best friend or bitterest enemy—or, in the course of a life relationship, both. At further degrees of segmentation, the ties are even more problematic and more conducive to situational shifts. Finally, the entire genealogical structure is complicated by polygyny. To be sure, plural marriage in Afghanistan is on the wane today, but many of the rural khans still indulge for motives that are political as well as romantic. The benefit of multiple alliance ties with other families, however, must be balanced against the increased potential for disruption at home. Once again, this potential is most readily actualized at the death of the father. When his heirs are only half-siblings, the struggle for authority can be all the harsher.

Nor does the principle of village residence provide institutions of specified authority. Many villages are merely spatial expressions of the same segmentary pattern described above. Others, to complicate matters further, incorporate members of more than one ethnic group, each with its own native language and endogamous marriage preference. The affairs of each such cluster within a village are focused on its own mosque, where discussions of community interest typically follow daily prayers. Each mosque, therefore, has its own *majles* or "council" to which every extended family supplies a *rish safed* or "elder" (literally, "white beard"). The majles is not, however, a truly formal institution with specified rules of membership and procedure. Rather, it consists of a loose collective of more or less politically important individuals who interact frequently in a variety of contexts and usually achieve consensus in an informal manner. More to the point, there is no fixed status of leader. This same majles arrangement recurs when representatives of the various intravillage mosque groups assemble for larger-scale discussions. Indeed, it reproduces itself on the ever-larger scale of valley, region, and even nation.

Always, however, the principle of residence is beset by the same problem of unspecified authority. Obviously some individuals have more of it than others—but not on account of a well-defined investiture process and, consequently, for only as long as they can manipulate changing circumstances to their own advantage. This classic problem is as yet unalleviated by recent government attempts to regularize its dealings with rural villages through the appointment of *arbabs* or "headmen." As a mediational figure, the arbab is responsible for registering births, marriages, and deaths with the government, for bringing serious disputes to government attention, and for facilitating government taxation and conscription. Typically, however, each village—certainly each group of villages—has more than one available arbab from whom potential clients can choose, and the problem of ultimate authority remains as unsettled as ever.

The principle of social class is weakly developed and supplies no institutions of political authority. No sense of caste exists here.[4] The formal stratification of earlier Central Asian khanates failed to survive their collapse. An effective end was put to slavery in the late nineteenth century. The associations of craft and trade that characterize contemporary towns do not extend to the occupationally unspecialized countryside. Wealthy khans sometimes find it expedient to make the claim that "we are all peasant farmers (*dehqan*) here." Such, self-evidently, is not the case, and more candid informants (with less to lose) usually present a three-tiered model with control over land (much, little, and none) as the criterion. There are, however, no names for these vaguely defined classes. Lacking institutional reality, they provide no effectual means for the exercise of authority. Far more typical than cooperation among status equals is their competition for the same scarce resources.

Islam, of course, is a central factor in cultural life, and virtually all aspects of existence testify to its pervasive influence. In this sense, it rightfully can be called "the strongest unifying force in Afghan society."[5] Its capacity for providing a unity of norms is more than offset,

however, by its failure to structure institutions through which authority can work. The Sunni denomination to which most northerners
adhere has no clerical hierarchy.[6] Although certain religious practi-
tioners in both Kabul and other cities are generally accorded special
status, no formal set of relationships stretches across the country. On
Fridays and holidays, members of several local mosques may congregate at a more elaborate one in what amounts to a rite of larger-scale
community organization. Otherwise, however, each congregation is
on its own, and its *mullah* has no authority beyond its social boundaries. Even within them the mullah is not necessarily a man of
authority in mundane matters.[7] Often he is a person of minimal
wealth who depends for a livelihood on richer and more powerful
individuals. Many khans still employ private mullahs whose presence
endows their patrons with a normatively approved aura of piety.

Family, residence, class, religion—all of these are important factors in day-to-day life, but none specify authority beyond a minimal
level. Instead their political significance can better be gauged in
terms of idiom. These social principles undoubtedly provide much
structure to existence, but they also afford a structural language
whereby individuals wheel and deal. Brother will side with brother
because, they both state as a matter of course, the fraternal tie
between them is inviolable. As circumstances change, however, so
too do the interests of each man, and sometimes these interests
become impossible for even sons of the same father to reconcile.
Then brother will oppose brother because, each may state (but only
in the unfortunate event that the breach becomes public), the other
is a *kaffir* or infidel.

In the absence of institutions that specify authority, this critical element is vested instead in individuals who cast themselves as leaders
and bolster their claims by the acquisition of followers. These men,
insofar as their claims are successful, become known as khans. As a
key linguistic element in Afghan concepts of prestige, the term itself
merits discussion. Its etymology is Central Asian, and its usage in
Afghanistan derives from the thirteenth-century invasions of Chingiz
(Khan) and his successors. Since that era it has been used to describe
a variety of authority-oriented statuses: some relatively institutionalized in unusual circumstances of political stability; others much less
so in typical conditions of institutional weakness. In the time of steppe-
pastoral empires, the honorific of khan was reserved for the paramount ruler. The disintegration of these empires, however, gradually
led to the current semantic use described by Barth for Swat Pathans:

> The title khan, even apart from its formal courtesy use, does not
> denote incumbency of any formal office. There is no organized
> hierarchy of offices to be filled by successive pretenders. The title
> merely implies a claim to authority over others. . . .[8]

It is the "claim to authority"—forever dependent upon claimant reputation—that lies, side by side with playful fun, at the center of all buzkashi.

Nowadays, the term khan is variously applied. Especially in rural society (but once again, significantly, at the highest Head-of-State level in the national elite), khan is appended as a suffix to the ascribed names of politically important men: Ramatullah Khan, Serajuddin Khan, or (the first President of the Republic) Mohammed Daoud Khan. This nomination is informal. No position in contemporary politics automatically conveys the institutionalized title of khan. Instead, the suffix is appended as an honorific by general consensus to represent general status. The nomination is marked by no ritual occasion and entails no specific authority. A khan, rather, is someone whose political recognition is general: the more general the recognition, the greater the khan.

Such recognition comes in the form of allegiance from other individuals who perceive such a patron-client relationship to be to their best advantage. Relatively unfettered by corporate obligations, such followers tend to come and go from situation to situation. Once again, Barth provides a ready description:

> Followers seek leaders who offer them the greatest advantages and the most security. With this aim they align themselves behind a rising leader who is successfully expanding his property and field of influence. In contrast, the followers of leaders who are on the defensive suffer constant annoyance from members of expanding groups. Under the pressure they tend to abandon their old leaders and seek protection and security elsewhere. Leaders are thus forced to engage in a competitive struggle. A position of authority can be maintained only through a constant struggle for the control of the sources of authority.[8]

The common term for such an aggregation of dependents, oriented towards a khan and maintained by his reputation, is *qaum*. The phrase *yak adam-i-quamdar ast*—"he's a man possessed of a qaum"—is used in summary form to explain political prominence with the implication that no more need be said. In its narrower sense, qaum refers to the whole hierarchy of segmentary descent groups extending upwards from the nuclear family to the ethnic totality. The ultimate weakness of such descent groups for guaranteeing social relationships has led, however, to a wide range of usages. Pierre Centlivres provides a comprehensive definition of qaum in his account of Khulm, a sizeable and ancient oasis town on the northern plains:

> Le term indigène pour groupe ethnique est qawm, mais le mot possède une extension beaucoup plus vaste, il designe en fait l'ensemble d'un group par rapport a ce qui lui est extériéure;

> dans son sens le plus restreint, il est utilisé pour la famille patril-
> inéaire; on l'emploi aussi pour désigner les gens de la même rue,
> du même métier, du quartier ou on habite, qawm-e guzar, la
> région naturelle, qawm-e turkestan, la groupe ethnique, qawm-e
> uzbek, qawm-e arab, et enfin parfois la nationalité.[10]

This vagueness of definition reflects the inherently situational nature of qaums. Lacking truly corporate group structure, they are organized instead around central khan individuals.

Thus the operative unit of social analysis is the individual himself, and the appropriate perspective that of network theory. As pioneered by John Barnes and synthesized more recently by others,[11] this approach understands social experience as a process rather than a system. Social relations are temporary rather than permanent, flexible rather than fixed. Success in social undertakings comes less through moral rectitude than through influential friends. Man is less a passive recipient of social fate than an active entrepreneur "who builds and manages an enterprise for the pursuit of profit in the course of which he innovates and takes risks."[12] In this sense, he is ultimately embarked on a course of lonely heroics in which, because of inevitable flux, he can never rest secure. Event follows event, and political closure never comes.

At the core of a khan-oriented aggregation are members of his own residential family for whom he serves in all respects as patriarch. Fortified by sentiments of household loyalty, these individuals constitute a truly corporate group and supply their senior male member with his most secure assistance. Theirs is a shared existence, and the density of relationships among the family members— as well as their individual ties to its leader—all but guarantees lifelong cooperation. With collateral branches of the same agnatic descent group, authority is more problematic, but a powerful khan tends by definition to be a man whose leadership provides sufficient benefits to cousins for them to accept him as paramount. The greater the khan, the wider the range of agnatic segments which subordinate themselves to him. At each successive stage of segmentation, however, the subordination becomes more vulnerable to recalculation.

Still very much under the direct influence of the khan, if unmotivated by family sentiment, are other individuals in his employ: household servants, stable grooms, and agricultural laborers. Less closely bound are nearby villagers for whom the khan accepts a nebulous but, especially in emergencies, very real sense of responsibility. Here again, the wider the geographical range encompassed by this relationship, the more ultimately powerful the khan. Finally, the successful khan has a stock of relationships with urban-based specialists, both governmental and commercial. These are ordinarily kept in reserve, bolstered from time to time by small favors, but for the most part allowed to lie dormant until some special need arises. In recent decades many rural khans have developed commercial interests in town, and for them the new urban networks are all the more important.

For the country-based khan and his followers, the primary scarce resources remain land, water, livestock, and—in a very real, but obviously different, sense—women. All four are vital, easily lost, and endlessly troublesome. All land not belonging to the government or to the *waqf* religious trust is privately owned, and everyone in a local community has some sense of whose land is whose. The absence, however, of precise survey and standardized documentation leads to disputes that are pursued through self-help. For all landholders, large and small alike, there is a constant need for vigilance against encroachment. Only such watchfulness and a forceful appearance of potential response can prevent predation. With water it is much the same: a basic insufficiency and therefore a constant threat of trouble. The fragile irrigation networks are controlled at their nodes by flimsy barrages of brush and mud. In springtime snowmelt from the mountains makes careful regulation unnecessary, but by late summer in an average year the situation becomes critical. A locally appointed *mirab* or "master of water" establishes timetables for consumption, but the potential for abuse is again limited only by a general impression of strength. Livestock are easily stolen from those too weak to defend them. It is women, however, who are widely considered the most volatile cause for serious dispute. Without control over female reproductive services, a man can have no sons (to assist in economic activity, to act as the core of political support, and to provide security in old age) and no daughters (to be married outside the nuclear family and thus to provide both bridewealth and affinal alliance). With their sexuality generally considered unmanageable, women are secluded as much as possible from all but the narrowest circle of family males. Here they serve as the primal embodiments of masculine honor. A man may suffer the loss of material property and still keep the core of his self-respect intact. Mere suspicion, on the other hand, of illicit access to his women requires an overt response: immediate and extreme.

In a purely economic sense, therefore, control over these scarce resources—land, water, livestock, and (somewhat more mystically) women—constitutes the main source of political authority. Whoever controls the means of production can buy compliance, and power without wealth is all but impossible.

Ultimately, however, another question presents itself. How, precisely, are these economic sources of authority controlled? Boundary lines are vague, irrigation barrages are flimsy, sheep are easily led away, and women are considered helplessly vulnerable in their innate sexuality. Virtually everyone, even more to the point, is a potential predator. Obviously, some sort of deterrent is necessary.

In rural Afghanistan, where no central government can guarantee security, that deterrent takes the form of the khan-centered qaum. That Hajji Yusuf Khan has a qaum of such-and-such followers is general knowledge, and would-be predators are discouraged accordingly. For the khan, however, the problem is that such support remains basically ephemeral. How can supporters best be attracted and, once attracted, held? In a continuous flux of events where group institutions are weakly defined, the greatest resource is individual reputation.

Hence the pervasive importance which everyone in society attaches to "name." To be sure, the stakes are less romantic and not so large in scale as in the Kurroglou legend. Palaces and princesses have faded from the rural scene, but reputation continues as the ultimate source of political authority. As a concept it has, in effect, two dimensions. One—*hisiyat* or "character"—describes the normative set of characteristics which serve as idioms for the public expression of alliance. The other—*e'tibar* or "credit"—reflects the harder-headed calculations that underlie such statements.

Khans are said, first of all, to possess hisiyat/character in the behavioral display of piety, generosity, and wisdom. The pervasiveness of Islam in everyday life allows for countless demonstrations of piety. Some are free of material cost: the daily prayers, the profession of faith, the annual Ramazan fast. Others, however, are more costly, and it is here that reputations for hisiyat are made on the basis of public observation: the gift of alms to the poor when men gather to pray, the pilgrimage to Mecca from which one returns with the new appellative *hajji*, the endowment of a mosque which subsequently bears the donor's name, the employment of one's own mullah who travels with his patron to ritual occasions. Generosity likewise assumes many forms, which range from the universal offer of tea to far grander gestures: the provision of great feasts such as accompany buzkashi games or the gift of prize horses. Indeed, the entire buzkashi occasion—at whatever level of society—is generally understood as an expression of sponsor generosity. Finally, wisdom is cited as a positive aspect of character. The wise man appreciates the reality of fate but is more than a fatalist. He listens well, talks little, learns much, bides his time, considers his options, and acts. He is deliberate rather than rash, purposeful rather than frivolous. He is dependable.

Social relationships not ascribed by descent ties are often phrased for public consumption in the various idioms of hisiyat. An individual may have many "friends" who are drawn to him by some stated combination of piety, generosity, and wisdom. Of the three, wisdom comes closest to that other, less purely virtue-oriented aspect of reputation: e'tibar. If hisiyat testifies to character, e'tibar expresses credit. E'tibar is often used in a financial sense. A man with e'tibar is certain to pay his financial debts and so can be loaned money without worry. More pertinent is the additional sense of political credit. Here e'tibar is at the center of the obsessive concern for reputation. The khan with political e'tibar can call on the services of supporters to help him in whatever enterprise. Their support is rendered in the dual expectation that (1) the enterprise will succeed and that (2) they will benefit somehow in return. In the case of some acquisitive move, their benefit may be directly realized in a share of the spoils. More commonly, it is deferred and takes quite unrelated form. In many cases, the less powerful clients of a khan are expected to serve him as a condition of their subordinate relationship. Whichever way, supporters extend political credit precisely to that person whose prospects hold the most for them. This calculation, of course, is reckoned in terms of impressions: how has so-and-so fared in the past, and what resources does he command in the present? The khan with e'tibar can never control the future completely. His reputation for political competence, however, suffices to make tomorrow appear somewhat more predictable.

Reputation is actually discussed on two levels. In an overt sense, much of the conversation that dominates social moments takes the form of narrative stories about persons who are either present themselves or are known to those present. As exploits are recounted and reinterpreted, their characters inevitably assume new dimensions. The story is told about how Nasrullah Khan of the Uzbek Lakai was the man who finally settled that boundary squabble by the river. Heads nod in confirmation as mental notes are made.

Less obviously, words like khan, hisiyat, e'tibar, and nam recur and combine as important items in a stylized sort of reputational talk which goes on among Afghans virtually all the time. Even in the most apparently apolitical conversation, reputational allusions constitute a kind of second level of dialogue. References to persons not present often evoke brief evaluative phrases that communicate little or no substance but add to the totality of personal image. Not surprisingly, religion offers the most comprehensive idiom. *"Khub Musselman ast"*—"He's a good Muslim"—has connotations far beyond matters of piety. If his name is mentioned, a powerful man may be described in passing as "a good Muslim" and "a servant of his qaum." Even when (as is usually the case) such references do not develop into fuller-scale stories, they bolster the reputations of their individual referents.

Indeed, the entire fabric of day-to-day life entails an obsessive concern for impressions. Everyone who participates in the public domain is involved as both actor and spectator. No event is without its potential for political connotations, and their subtleties are observed with intense interest. Some contexts, of course, are overtly political, and lessons there are relatively plain even for an outsider. At every majles council, for instance, discussions are held and decisions are made (even if their effect is to defer decision). It is fairly easy to tell in such instances who has the measure of authority (even here, however, the most influential speaker may, in fact, operate as a front man for some more powerful and utterly silent khan). In less obviously political events, no more than a kinesic hint may indicate who's who. Virtually any encounter between two men reveals the nature of their relationship in a set of stereotypical gestures. Intensity shows in the closeness of embrace, which ranges from thrice repeated hugs to a perfunctory handshake. Relative status is expressed in degree of movement: The superior person remains still while his subordinate pays him homage with whatever spatial adjustments are necessary. No words need be exchanged; the verbal conventions of greeting, in fact, often suggest symmetry. Canny observers look instead to the subtler, but truer and universally recognized language of movement.

As political relationships shift across time, so also do their concrete manifestations in everyday life. From the outside it is tempting to conclude that here is a political field largely, if not altogether, lacking in structure. One concedes some truth to that nineteenth-century evaluation in which "this continuous struggle of agitation, intrigue, perfidy, and dominion seems to be an innate necessity to a khan."[13] Authority, however, certainly does exist, in individuals if not in formal statuses or permanent corporations. So does structure, but informal rather than institutional, and dynamic rather than fixed. For the clearest illustration of this structure—as it exists at any moment in time—one need only walk through the gates of a khan compound and into his sumptuous guesthouse.

In a landscape of political impressions, the compound of a powerful khan dominates all other works of man. Coated with the same brown mud, its walls rise well above those of lesser persons: 30 feet or more from bottom to top, and five feet thick at the base. Other architectural features testify to status: a second story to some interior building looming against the skyline; a bulge on the western side indicating the *mihrab* of a private mosque; and perhaps a newly drilled well, complete with concrete shaft and iron windlass, where village women draw water twice a day hard by the gates of their patron. By day these thick wooden gates are swung outwards on massive hinges; a male servant (a guest house attendant or perhaps the stable groom) will bar them at sunset.

Once through the gates the visitor stands in an open courtyard. At its far side rises a similarly formidable interior wall that divides the compound into its two spheres: public and private (see figure 2-1). Behind this wall remain the family women, with whom unrelated males are forbidden all contact. Nor are any inquiries made, even the most perfunctory; for the visitor this secluded domain may as well not exist.

Instead his attention is directed at once to the champion buz-kashi horses tethered conspicuously between gates and guesthouse. With their erect heads and powerful frames, it is impossible not to admire them and unthinkable not to say so. In return, the visitor may be given details of pedigree or performance. Finally, he is led across the compound to the guesthouse itself—in the case of a really powerful khan, an entirely separate edifice with veranda, lavatory, and at least one spacious room. The visitor adds his shoes to a pile by the door and walks through it to face an assembly of quickly attentive men.

Even for the foreigner, who—at least at the outset of his stay—does not count socially, such an entrance can be somewhat unnerv-ing. For the ongoing member of society, it is imbued with much greater significance. Whatever the structure of political relationships at this time, his position in it is about to be overtly revealed.

Lavishly furnished with carpets and cushions woven in red and black Turkman motifs, the guest room is already full of men seated in a rectangle with their backs to the walls. It is this rectangular floor plan, imposed by architecture and fundamentally different from the egalitarian roundness of meetings held on the ground in front of a mosque, that forces a revelation of structure (see figure 2-2). In the subtle, but universally acknowledged, language of proxemics, the rel-ative status of each individual is reflected in where he sits.

The men already in the room are seated accordingly. Highest-sta-tus individuals sit *bala* or "high" along the narrow end of the rectan-gle farther from the door. The highest-status individual of them all occupies the center spot. The long sides of the rectangular room are lined with men of progressively lower status with the very lowest at the end nearer the door (*payan*). Thus the newcomer can tell with one look who is who in relative status. His role in the process, how-ever, is far from merely passive. Like all those who have arrived before him, he too must now find—and be found—his proper place. Conversation has abated to a whisper, and for the next few moments this one man is the focus of attention.

First the new arrival starts at the doorway and walks around the entire room exchanging greetings with each man in turn. These exchanges are often as perfunctory as they are obligatory: a hand-shake and the murmured phrases known collectively as *jur personi* or "asking after health." Personal elaboration is generally absent. On the contrary, exchanges may last less than five seconds with no eye contact. At this stage, the one most significant element is kinesic, the extent to which each of the already seated men gets to his feet in greeting the newcomer. In most cases they simply extend their hands from a seated position or perhaps rise to one knee. For a high-status arrival, however, they may stand individually as he tours the room,

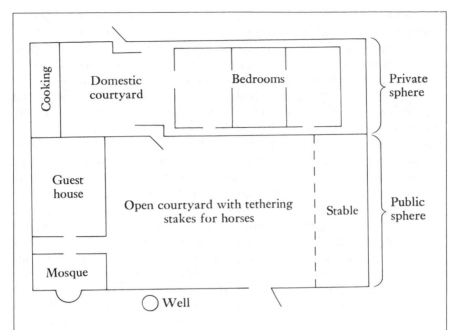

Figure 2-1   Architectural Plan of Typical Khan Compound

Figure 2-2   Floor of Typical Compound Guesthouse

or even in extreme instances remain standing together as a group until he has completed the circuit and takes a seat himself.

The location of that seat is an even clearer indication of status. The introductory round has taken only a few moments. The new arrival will sit, however, in the same position for hours, and that spatial situation will reflect his status and, indeed, define his role. At the end of his tour, the newcomer turns to face the room once more. Some already seated man then shifts his body slightly, making room immediately above him, and invites the newcomer to sit, in effect, higher than him. This invitation is made all the more gracious by the use of whatever honorific title the newcomer may have and so is phrased, "Sit up here, hajji sahib" or "arbab sahib" or whatever. It is always a peer or near peer who makes the offer. For a clear superior to do so would be preposterous; for a clear inferior to do so would be presumptuous. For a status equal to do so, however, is to display graciousness towards others and confidence in self. Despite its literal appearance, the invitation is not really an acknowledgement that the newcomer is higher in status. If anything, the reverse is ever so faintly suggested: that the already seated man can claim to influence where the newcomer sits. The newcomer typically responds with perfunctory protestations to the effect that the other man should be higher, but finally takes the seat as indicated. If more than one man offers to make room, the new arrival, of course, has a choice.

Wherever he sits, he proceeds to make one more set of greeting gestures. From his newly seated posture, he nods towards two or three of the highest-status men, places his right hand over his heart in a stylized expression of sincerity, maintains eye contact, and again murmurs a couple of jur personi phrases. It is a signal that he is now both seated in the gathering and situated in the structure of relationships.

There is never the smallest hint of contention while this process is underway. No man ever makes an overt claim to a better seat than he is offered. To do so would be considered impossibly bad form, rude in its own right, and plainly indicative of insecurity. For someone who perceives himself slighted, it is far better to seem unperturbed at the time and to ponder future implications behind an impassive face.

These rectangular gatherings diagram political structure. That its statuses are informal and its corporate sense poorly developed make the structure itself no less real. With authority vested in individuals and reckoned in terms of their reputations, politics is fundamentally an impressionistic process. Ultimately, power is as power seems, and the "man with a qaum" is necessarily the "man with a name." The structure is reflected and, inevitably, altered by the experiential flow of events. In this expanded sense, all of life is an arena with political implications. Most of life, however, is inherently mundane and even routine.

Guesthouse gatherings provide clear representations of the authority structure, but these are both private and, for the most part, orderly. Mud walls and emotional controls limit the potential for drama and volatility. Crises, of course, do erupt through the calm but brittle shell of daily experience. These can entail outright fighting, and life then "becomes a buzkashi." Somewhere in the ambiguous middle—between the ordinary and the critical—lies the game itself: part cooperation and part competition, part play and part politics, and wholly engrossing like nothing else in Afghanistan.

NOTES

[1] Marco Polo, *Travels*, ed. Sir Henry Yule (London: John Murray, 1903), p. 151.

[2] Ferrier, Joseph Pierre, *Caravan Journeys and Wanderings in Persia, Afghanistan, Turkistan, and Beloochistan* (London: John Murray, 1857), p. 204.

[3] Vambery, A., *Travels in Central Asia* (London: John Murray, 1864), p. 244.

[4] In Kunduz Province and certain other northern areas, an ethnic group called Jugi is despised so generally as to seem almost caste-like. Dark-complexioned, Jugis themselves claim to have come from Arabia via Bokhara, but others attribute Indian origins. The notion of intermarriage with Jugis is spurned by members of other groups. Informants do insist, however, that there are no formal prohibitions against contact. Significantly, the most popular town crier in Kunduz buzkashi (see chapter 3) was a Jugi. With little status to lose, he (and later two close relatives) could afford both to sing other men's praises and to act the buffoon on horseback. Habibullah Jugi is not to be confused with Habib the great chapandaz. Both, however, befriended me, and the town crier *par excellence* remains a close pal.

[5] Newell, Richard S., *The Politics of Afghanistan* (Cornell University Press: Ithaca, 1972), p. 26.

[6] This lack of clerical structure among Sunni Muslims in Afghanistan stands in sharp and politically feckless contrast to the situation of Shi'ite Iran, with its powerful ayatollahs and the tradition of an imminent imam.

[7] The status *of pir* or "saint" exists in northern Afghanistan, but my research suggests nothing like the political power ascribed to their counterparts in Swat by Fredrik Barth ("Political Leadership Among Swat Pathans," in *Friends, Followers, and Factions*, ed. Steffan W. Schmidt, Laura Gauste, Carl H. Londe, and James C. Scott [Berkeley: University of California Press, 1977]). Islam provides a common idiom for political discourse in which enemies are typically characterized as "bad Muslims" or "unbelievers," but religious eminence is generally not the paramount factor in personal prestige and subsequent authority.

[8] Barth, "Political Leadership," p. 215.

[9] Ibid., p. 214.

[10] The indigenous term for the group is *qawm*, but the word has a far wider meaning inasmuch as it designates a group as a whole as compared to anyone outside it; in its most restricted sense, it is used for the patrilineal

family; it is also used to designate people living on the same street, of the same trade (profession), the block where one lives, *qawm-e guzar*; the natural region, *qawm-e turkestan*; the ethnic group, *qawm-e uzbek, qawm-e arab;* and finally sometimes nationality. Centlivres, Pierre, *Un Bazaar d'Asie Centrale* (Weisbaden: L. Riechert, 1972), pp. 158–159.

[11]For the seminal article in network theory see Barnes, J. A., "Class and Committees in a Norwegian Island Parish," *Human Relations 1* (1954): 39–58

[12]Boissevain, Jeremy, *Friends of Friends* (Oxford: Basil Blackwell, 1974), p.147

[13]Ferrier, "Caravan Journeys," p. 204.

3

THE BUZKASHI TOOI

And then a swarm of wandering horse, who came
From afar, and a more doubtful service own'd.
　　　　　　　　—Matthew Arnold, "Sohrab and Rustam "

Towards the end of November, the yearly cycle of agriculture in northern Afghanistan enters its least active phase. Fields lie unattended, canal water freezes, and livestock huddle under the lee of enclosure walls. Some work continues in the provision of fodder for sheep, the repair of farm implements, and for women the same continuous round of domestic chores. For men, however, the winter months traditionally constitute at least a partial respite from the press of livelihood demands. Now they can turn instead to other matters: occasions which, they say, are more purely social and more in line with their shouq interests. Winter is the time for toois and buzkashi.

The term tooi has two semantic dimensions. In the narrower sense, it means a rite of passage: either circumcision or marriage. More widely, it refers to whatever festivity accompanies such a rite. These two components of tooi activity are kept procedurally separate. The rite of passage is an essentially sequestered event with participation limited to family members: males and females, kin and affines. The festivity, especially when it is featured by buzkashi, occurs publicly and incorporates much broader participation.

Not all toois are spectacularly festive. Most men would relish the sponsorship role, but only a small minority, the khans, can afford its costs. Nor, it must be noted, do all men called "khan" still sponsor buzkashi toois. In the more exclusively rural past, so informants maintain, the buzkashi tooi was a universal aspect of khan activity.

Now some khans with urban ties claim they simply lack the shouq and channel their resources in less traditional directions.

In the countryside, however, buzkashi toois still highlight the otherwise drab winter months, and many khans with their retinues travel from festival to festival. Once again, the essential question occurs: What is it that's going on here? And once again, the answer can best be phrased in terms of frame ambiguity. Self-evidently, the tooi as a whole, like the buzkashi it incorporates, exists for the sake of fun, friendship, and recreation. The anthropologist is quick to recognize it as a ceremony of integration; past is linked culturally with present, and men are linked socially with one another. That the principals at a tooi are typically khans, however, makes the existence of a second frame of political connotation all but inevitable. On no other occasion do so many khans from such a wide geographical range interact for so prolonged a period and in such volatile circumstances as at a buzkashi tooi. Here, as always among khans, the locus of authority is at stake, and the entire tooi process can alternatively be interpreted—if not generally acknowledged—as a political microcosm. From first to last, it constitutes a public arena whose events can be taken as evidence of who exacts compliance from whom. The ambiguity of games extends throughout the tooi experience as the frame of each individual shifts back and forth between "for fun" and "for real."

For purposes of conceptual convenience, the flow of tooi activity is divided here into three phases: preparation, festivities, and aftermath. A final section in this chapter presents a pair of toois; the first memorably successful, the second much less so.

PREPARATION

The preparation phase of a buzkashi tooi is both elaborate and problematic. Much of its concern is with material resources: the procurement of goods, the cooking of foods, the readying of guest houses. This study, however, concentrates on human resources and the issue of authority over them. More precisely, it focuses on the process in which decisions are made and implemented. This decision process has four steps of consideration and reconsideration. All four revolve around the same individual: the *tooi-wala* or (would-be) "festival sponsor." Each step is successively more extensive in social scope, more open to public observation, and as such more consequential in the all-important domain of reputation:

1. consideration by the tooi-wala alone;
2. consideration by the tooi-wala and his closest associates;
3. consideration by the tooi-wala, his closest associates, and

those whom he attempts to enlist as household servants (*khesh*); and

4. consideration by the tooi-wala, his closest associates, and those whom he attempts to enlist as subsidiary hosts (*mehmandars*).

Each of these steps constitutes a problematic event. Each is concerned with a set of decisions whose outcome is unsure until it actually occurs. Even then, the decisions made at one step are only tentative. Despite the appearance of permanence that the decision makers attempt to impart to them, they may be revised by other decision makers in the subsequent step. Taken together, the process represents a start of the third-order game (see chapter 1) in which participants struggle for control over the tooi as a whole.

At the center of this process, like a lonely hero in a politically perilous landscape, stands the tooi-wala. Every tooi has a private sponsor, and while it is conceivable that two or more men may share this role, such partnership is rare. Far more typical is the practice of individual sponsorship by a khan whose son is to be circumcised or married. Such initiative, however normatively apolitical, entails great potential for reputation: its gain and its loss. A successful tooi "raises the name" of its tooi-wala; failure results in reputational fall.

Throughout the tooi an essential difficulty faces the tooi-wala. Simply stated, he needs the help of other persons who, potentially at least, are his rivals and whose support, therefore, is never absolutely secure. Any tooi, and especially the sort of buzkashi tooi that will render his name truly memorable, requires not only his own efforts but also those of many other individuals. Hundreds, even thousands, of invited guests must be fed and sheltered with elaborate hospitality. The buzkashi game must itself be properly supervised. The whole enterprise must be maintained with an appearance of effortless control for the two, three, four, or five days of its duration. Here, as in the fourth-order game of "real-world" politics, a khan needs a qaum.

This tooi qaum, like its mundane counterpart, is a complex but unstable structure: oriented in network fashion around its central figure, recruited through various principles (kinship, affinity, authentic friendship, economic dependence, and political expediency), and situationally activated for this one enterprise. That its core consists for the most part of close patrilineal relatives does little to give it a true sense of corporate group; even for these agnatic kinsmen, the focal point in this context is the tooi-wala himself, and commitment to him varies inversely with remoteness of relationship. For the others—affines, friends, clients, and allies—the ties to the tooi-wala are even more tenuous. Indeed, the entire qaum of supporters for a tooi-wala amounts, after Barnes, to an "action-set" whose very existence is realized only as a means towards some specific enterprise.[1]

The tooi qaum, lastly, has a developmental quality: it grows—or, rather, its central figure seeks to have it grow—as the decision process goes from step to step and incorporates ever more participants. At each step of qaum ramification, however, the support of these participants becomes more problematic, and the attendant risks become more public.

All four steps in the preparation phase deal, in effect, with the same set of decisions:

1. whether there is to be a buzkashi tooi at all;
2. when it is to be held;
3. for how long it is to be held;
4. who will act as servants at the residence of the tooi-wala;
5. who will act as subsidiary hosts for the invited guests;
6. who those invited guests will be; and
7. which guests will stay with which hosts.

Two concerns loom over the entire preparation phase. The first, self-evidently, has to do with the content of these seven decisions. Equally important, if less immediately obvious, is the matter of who controls the decision process. The outcome in both cases is far from predictable. For the tooi-wala, the ideal would consist of decisions in favor of the largest and longest tooi ever known with complete support from the most extensive set of supporters who were themselves individuals of the greatest prestige. He himself, furthermore, would exercise unilateral authority in all respects. What actually happens is much more complicated.

The first step for a would-be tooi-wala takes the form of private consideration. There must, initially, be a son of suitable age for circumcision or marriage. Supposedly, it is the rite of passage that prompts the festivity, and not vice versa. The age range for both rites is quite broad, however, and a father with several young sons (quite common especially for the largely polygynous khans) can thus initiate the tooi process whenever he deems it most opportune. At first he considers the situation in the ultimate privacy of his own mind: his reputation (name), his potential support (qaum), and the appropriateness of a tooi initiative to his present circumstances. The wise man is deliberate and keeps his own counsel; no social shame can attach to the negative outcomes when the knowledge of them is limited to their instigator alone. In the realm of reputational politics, initiatives are risky only when they become public. Only after careful calculation does the would-be tooi-wala consult his closest associates.

This second step consists of dyadic conversations between him and several men whose support he believes to be most secure. These closest associates are generally near agnates (brothers and father's brothers' sons); only a khan whose authority extended at least that far would presume to attempt tooi sponsorship. Breadth of support is likewise important, even at this early step, and some influential friend outside the family may be enlisted. Trust is the critical criterion; the tooi preparations must still remain confidential lest they never materialize any further. Such a failure could always be dismissed by the unsuccessful tooi-wala as a recreational matter of no consequence, but his frustration is liable to be framed by others in serious political terms: that the enterprise failed because its sponsor lacked sufficient authority. These new confidants must be trusted to keep the matter to themselves.

Typically, one of them is asked to serve as *tooi-bashi* or, in effect, general manager of the tooi. This role is critical to the entire enterprise. The tooi-bashi performs as a kind of transactional alter ego for the tooi-wala. The pervasive concern for impressions is reflected in the need for this executive figure. Throughout the tooi, its sponsor endeavors to maintain the culturally approved demeanor of pure hospitableness, and thus to seem above practical concerns such as mobilization of support, administration of resources, and settlement of disputes. His manner must always remain calmly confident that all will go well: that, in other words, he has turned a problematic process into a predictable system with himself in effortless authority over it. To convey this impression, he needs someone to do the dirty work for him.

The enlistment of a tooi-bashi is typically phrased in the normative idiom of "best friend," but selection is inevitably based on pragmatic grounds as well. The ideal tooi-bashi, to quote one canny and eloquent informant, "does not steal the show, does not put the money in his pocket, knows how a tooi works from start to finish, and has a name so that others listen when he speaks."

If the consensus of these dyadic conversations is positive, the tooi-wala may gather his newly recruited supporters for an informal discussion. Now the whole set of tooi issues is considered once more, and previous agreements are once more vulnerable to revision. Such a meeting usually concentrates, however, on two lists of further supporters: the khesh members who (hopefully) will act as household servants at the tooi-wala residence, and the mehmandars who (hopefully) will act as subsidiary hosts. Once compiled, the lists then lead to the next two steps in tooi preparation.

If the first two steps were informal matters of private contemplation and dyadic conversation, each of the next two constitutes a well-defined event. Each entails invitations, occurs at a specific time and place, takes the form of an elaborate feast, and as such is essentially public. Each is successively riskier for the tooi-wala.

Of the two events, however, the third step (khesh) is both less elaborate in hospitality and less problematic in outcome. Khesh, in this sense, refers to those members of the sponsor's kindred (agnates and affines) whose assistance is necessary at his residence, the *tooi-khana*. There they will act as domestic servants: chopping wood, readying guest areas, serving food, washing dishes, and running errands. Their women, recruited through them, will work unseen in the private section of the tooi-khana compound.

First, however, these khesh members must be entertained. Only after a meal is the issue raised. As always, it is expressed in the idiom of friendship. Decisions already considered by the tooi-wala sponsor in the first two steps are now reconsidered. If his calculations of support were wrong, these reconsiderations may prove negative, with more serious consequences for the tooi-wala than if his enterprise had failed earlier. Here many more individuals are aware of that failure, and their confidentiality is less secure.

This third step, however, rarely poses insurmountable problems. Almost inevitably, the tooi-wala is a khan whose political status is unequalled in his kindred. In this sense he already exists as family patron, and his relationships with khesh members tend to be asymmetrical. What is phrased as a request often carries the force of a command. Once more, the issue depends on the extent of qaum authority.

One more step remains before the proposal of a tooi can become a reality. The tooi-wala must now gain the support of the mehmandars, who will provide accommodation for the (again hopefully) enormous number of guests in attendance at the tooi: not only the actual khan invitees but also their retinues. Thus the mehmandars must themselves be men of substance, that is, khans. This final step typically proves the most contentious. It entails the same familiar questions—what decisions are taken, and who controls that process—but now the participants are less likely to be mere subordinates of the tooi-wala. Their relationships to him usually represent a much more complex mixture of cooperation and competition.

Three factors determine the list of those invited to the mehmandar session. First, the mehmandars must reside enough near the buzkashi field (itself located as near as possible to the tooi-khana) so that they and their guests can go back and forth every day. Second, these subsidiary hosts must be of high enough status to provide suitable hospitality in the name of the tooi-wala. No sponsor would want a no-account as one of his hoteliers. Third, they must be sufficiently well-disposed towards the tooi-wala so that he can count on their support. This third criterion receives special deliberation: far better not to ask a khan at all than to have him refuse the invitation. Once these invitations are out the door, the tooi process has become truly public.

The invitations for the mehmandar session are issued for a date quite soon in the future: a week at the most, but more typically only a day or two. Three notions—an assumption, a hope, and a fear—

explain the speed of this process. The assumption is that during the agricultural off season the invitee will have no more pressing responsibilities. The hope is that other social plans will be altered in deference to the more important tooi. The fear is part of a more pervasive attitude towards the future in this situational society: that things left too long can go wrong. Relationships can shift, and what support the tooi-wala already has can quickly erode. From the khesh banquet to the end of a buzkashi tooi, less than two weeks usually elapse.

This time the invitations are written (perhaps by the compound mullah or a son who has been to school) and delivered on horseback. The already mobilized khesh members (and their unseen wives) prepare for the mehmandar feast. The tooi-wala, his tooi-bashi, and the other close supporters can only wait and hope for the best. How many mehmandar invitees will come and, once on hand, how they will behave—both of these eventualities lie in an unknowable future.

As the mehmandars arrive on the designated day, they are shown into the tooi-khana and go through the process of greeting and seating, which situates them in a spatial expression of current political structure. Their individual positions (bala and payan) will determine in part the roles they take in discussion. First, however, there is an initial expression of hospitality: each mehmandar has a small teapot, porcelain teacup, and dish of candies placed in front of him. The sentiment is reiterated throughout the day in word, deed, food, and drink. Whether its ethic of openhanded friendship can prevail in the decision process is another matter.

Conversation during this preliminary period is still generalized. The tooi-wala wonders to himself how many mehmandars are still on their way, but substantive business cannot wait forever. Finally, the topic that faces the gathering is recognized as such, and sociability turns to serious discussion. This shift is signaled by a direct address from as prominent an individual as can be recruited for the purpose. He may be the tooi-bashi or someone with even more status in the fourth-order game of "real-world" politics. Rarely, if ever, would the tooi-wala speak on his own behalf. To ask for support himself would be too blatant and, ultimately, too risky. Evasive replies in such an instance would too clearly suggest direct refusals, and the indispensable appearances of friendship would be harder to preserve.

Typically delivered from the prestigious bala end of the room, this speech is meant to mobilize support for the tooi and its sponsor. It formally announces the tooi and praises the tooi-wala for his generalized hisiyat virtues: his piety, his generosity, his wisdom. It may, more specifically, recall past favors to this or that beneficiary. References to e'tibar, the harder-nosed component of reputation concerned with political credit, are few and subtly phrased. In this process the speaker tries to extend the sense of sponsorship identity from the individual "I" of the tooi-wala to the collective "we" of everyone on hand. He seeks, in other words, to consolidate the "action" set qaum: "We are all friends of Hajji Aziz Khan (or, alternatively, all Uzbeks, Kunduzis, khans, Moslems, whatever) and we must work together to make our tooi great and famous." At the same time, of course, the speaker must also take care not to be carried away by collective sentiment which, if taken literally, would dilute the dominant authority of the tooi-wala.

At the close of this keynote address, the real discussion starts. Once more the basic decisions must be considered. Some are relatively easy to resolve; others can provoke enough conflict to abort the entire tooi. In order to encourage a cooperative ethic, the tooi-bashi introduces the less contentious issues first. The most basic decision—whether there is to be a tooi at all—appears already settled. The very presence of the mehmandars constitutes support, and there is no need for this item to be reviewed in any formal sense. Of course, conflict at whatever point later in the process can still wreck the entire enterprise. Two other decisions have likewise been tentatively settled beforehand: who will act as khesh servants and mehmandar hosts. Four decisions remain. All have already been considered by the tooi-wala, but the extent to which he can dictate them intact is extremely problematic.

Supposedly, these four issues are quite unrelated to politics, and expressions of disinterest are common at first. Thus, says a mehmandar, it makes no difference to him (1) when the tooi starts ("One day is as good as another to me"); (2) how long it lasts ("I am willing to accommodate my guests indefinitely"); (3) who is invited ("All you fellow mehmandars are my friends, and any friends of yours are friends of mine"); and (4) which of those guests stay in his house ("Among us fellow Moslems, all men are of equal status"). Supposedly, furthermore, it makes no difference whose authority controls the discussion.

Initial protestations notwithstanding, these four decisions are related to politics in varying degrees. The decision of when to schedule the tooi is least politically important, except in cases where toois are known to conflict. Then the issue for any khan is which tooi to support in which capacity. Somewhat more important is the decision of how long the tooi is to last and, as such, how much of their own resources—time, money, effort, and reputation—the individual mehmandars are willing to expend. More significant still is the decision of whom to invite as guests, and each mehmandar wants as many of his own "friends" as possible on the list. Most sensitive of all is the decision, usually left until last, of which guests will stay with which hosts, each of whom would ideally like the highest-status invitees to stay with him.

Both of the latter two decisions point to the fundamental importance of reputation. In compiling the guest list, the discussion proceeds valley by valley or, in greater detail, canal by canal across the
surrounding countryside. For a really large tooi, this survey of potential invitees can extend throughout most of northern Afghanistan.
Millions of men live in this area, and yet only a few hundred at most
are mentioned. This network of names, as informal as it is elitist,
seems eminently natural to its khan participants. One member of it,
more than a bit exasperated with my outsider simplemindedness,
explained the process succinctly:

> How do I know them? What do you mean, "How do I know
> them?" I know them. They are not peasants. These men have
> names. They have property. They have good lives. They have
> guest houses. They come and go, hosting and being hosted. Of
> course I know them. How would I not know them? It is the same
> in America. They have names. Kennedy. Kennedy. Kennedy.
> Kennedy. You know the name, don't you? Of course you do.
> Everyone knows it. He has a name.

With "name" as the fundamental concern, this mehmandar session
itches with potential for conflict. The tooi-wala and those closest to
him do all they can to exercise control. Almost certainly they will have
ventured to make the various decisions tentatively in advance; that the
tooi will start on this day and last for this long and have these guests
who will stay with these hosts. To the extent that his authority is paramount over the mehmandars, the tooi-wala can dictate these decisions
intact and enhance his control over the tooi as a whole. Otherwise, his
advance decisions may give way to open-ended discussions, degener-
ate into unmanageable bickering, and finally "become a buzkashi."

If control is not regained, the tooi is effectively finished. The necessary supporters become disgruntled and abandon the whole enterprise. For the tooi-wala, such an outcome can be quite serious. In
terms of resources—time, money, effort, and particularly reputation—his losses are greater and longer lasting than if the tooi had
failed at an earlier step. Even if control is regained, the memory of
chaos lingers. What can happen once can happen again, and erstwhile supporters begin to hedge their bets. If control is regained, but
by someone not directly associated with the sponsorship, then the
trouble has only begun: the tooi may continue, but with its locus of
authority dangerously uncertain.

With respect to recruitment of human resources, this fourth step
completes preparation for the tooi. If all has proceeded as planned,
the tooi-wala now has his support qaum. Its ultimate loyalty may
remain problematic, but at least the final set of invitations can now
go to the guests:

> The honored Sardar Mohammed Karim is invited to three days
> of buzkashi sponsored by Hajji Aziz Khan of Bowin on the occa-
> sion of the circumcision of his son Ghulam Hussein starting on
> Tuesday, the eleventh of Dalw, at eight o'clock in the morning.

Again these invitations are written by hand and delivered on
horseback, although messengers may travel by motorized transport
to more distant provinces. Again there is no guarantee that the
guests will actually come. The tooi-wala and his supporters will simply have to wait. In the meanwhile, attention finally turns towards
material preparations: food (vast quantities of sheep, rice, flour, tea,
sugar, candy, and oil), implements (cushions, pillows, trays, plates,
cups, and saucers), and finally, a pair of live two-year-old calves for
each intended day of buzkashi.

FESTIVITIES

Depending on the circumstances of travel (distance and means),
guests often leave home a day or more in advance and stay the nights
on route. Even the most important men used to travel by horseback,
and many still do so when bound for a buzkashi. Considering it
somewhat demeaning to sleep in wayside tea houses, every khan
seeks to create his own network of other khans with whom he can
always be sure of hospitality. Thus guests congregate with other
guests and proceed towards the tooi together. These aggregations
may remain more or less intact even after arrival and constitute
loose factions if serious disputes arise.

Each invitation bears only the name of a single invitee. It is
understood, however, that any guest may bring with him as many as
ten or fifteen other men: relatives by descent and marriage, co-resi-
dents of his home community, servants for himself and his horses,
and finally his chapandaz. In a much less purely recreational sense,
this retinue of "friends" also represents a private support contingent
ready for instant mobilization.

The arrival of guests on the first morning of a tooi is in many ways
similar to that at the earlier mehmandar meeting. This time, however,
the scale is much larger, as hundreds and sometimes thousands
come to be welcomed at the tooi-khana. The khans and their entourages enter the compound which by mid-morning is already teeming
with men. Now another, and even more massive, ceremonial meal is
hosted by the tooi-wala and consumed in informal shifts as the guests
arrive, eat, and ride on horseback to the nearby buzkashi field.

FINAL INVITATIONS. With the guest list finally organized, invitations are written
and dispatched. The worried sponsorship expressions tell of a tooi already
◄ in troubhe for lack of qaum support.

First, however, each invitee offers a gift known as *shenak*. Given in the name of friendship, shenak is handed personally and more or less privately to the tooi-wala or his tooi-bashi. Traditionally, it took the form of produce or, more memorably, of some status item: a rifle, a cloak, or a carpet. Now it usually comes in plain cash. Supposedly, the shenak prestation is optional and its amount is said by the tooi-wala to be unimportant: "Friendship is above money." In reality, however, shenak gifts are observed, remembered, and compared. Liberality enhances reputation. One Kunduz khan, for instance, "never gives less than 2,000 afghanis," and his arrival at a tooi is always accorded special attention. Significant prestige likewise accrues to whoever gives the largest shenak. It is not unknown for a status-conscious khan to delay his approach until almost noon and then to present what amounts, in effect, to the lowest possible highest shenak. In general, however, shenak amounts vary with the dyadic relationships between individual guests and the tooi-wala: the closer and more positive the relationship, the more generous the gift.

These shenak gifts can be critical for the tooi-wala in two respects. First, their total amount, kept a secret or distorted when smaller than expected, but leaked throughout the tooi when gratifyingly large, serves as an initial reflection of sponsor prestige. Common knowledge of a large shenak furthers the impression of tooi-wala authority. Second, this money covers part of the tooi costs. If his financial resources are already strained, the tooi-wala may have to depend on shenak to provide the prizes in buzkashi play. The size of these prizes, in turn, is one of the most indicative measures of sponsor performance.

With the guests arrived, the feast consumed, and the shenak transacted, it is time for the buzkashi—the first-order game—to begin. Preparations are in the past. Whether circumcision or marriage, the actual rite of passage remains a remote concern. From mid-morning until late afternoon on the two, three, or four days of play, buzkashi will occupy center stage.

The horsemen ride in informal bunches to a designated stretch of barren ground beyond the last irrigation canal. Play begins whenever someone from the tooi-khana brings the first calf carcass. Bled to death in accordance with ritual standards of Moslem propriety, it has then been completely decapitated. All four hooves have been severed so contestants will not cut their hands. Incisions between bone and tendon below the knee in the back legs make it easier for the calf to be grabbed off the ground. Depending on its weight and on the sort of game sought, the carcass may or may not have been eviscerated; a light calf makes for a running game with plenty of equestrian finesse, but a heavy calf, so the real aficionados say, reveals a more powerfully true sense of buzkashi superiority.

THE BUZKASHI CALF. Faced toward Mecca and bled to death with a perfunctory prayer, a calf is decapitated. Its hooves will be cut off to protect chapandazan hands.

Despite the stated invitation hour, there is no attempt to start at any set time, and play is usually ragged at first. Gradually, more and more khans arrive at the field with their retinues. The tooi-wala typically waits at home to welcome latecomers. Some of his khesh servants may likewise be concerned with household tasks. Otherwise, the entire male cast of tooi participants is on hand. By noon hundreds may have become thousands. The buzkashi form is traditional tudabarai. Everyone is on horseback.[2] Everyone, at least in theory, "has the right" to try for the carcass.

In practice, play tends to be dominated by the specialist chapandazan who ride the famed horses of their patrons. Physically powerful and distinctively dressed in cotton cloaks and fur-rimmed sheepskin hats called *telpaks*, these men embody buzkashi tradition. Their names and, in some cases, the names of their fathers are known across northern Afghanistan. As Khol Mohammed arrives at a game with fingers broken only a month ago, the older men remember his father Ibrahim, who died of a gangrenous stomach ruptured by his own saddle horn. It was a heavy calf, they say, really more of a cow, and Ibrahim impaled himself rather than let go. Like father, like son: both men are known as *zamin-gir* chapandazan whose forte is in the act of getting the calf from the ground. Other riders, quicker and perhaps more cunning, are called *chakka-gir* for their skill at stealing a carcass at top speed.

For all his physical power and heroic allure, the chapandaz himself seldom has much political stature. Traditionally, he shares some sort of qaum affiliation with the khan whose horse he rides, and exists very much as a client at the beck and call of his patron. His own extended family may own some land on which the chapandaz labors like any other farmer for most of the year. Only in the winter buzkashi season, heralded by the October announcement of the Kabul buzkashi championship, does he become transformed from typical peasant bound by the soil to charismatic personification of the equestrian past.[3]

Massively mounted on the best horses and distinguished by their telpak hats, the chapandazan struggle for the calf carcass and occupy the middle ground of a roughly concentric mass which moves with the flow of play. Around them on every side are the khans and their higher-status retainers. More socially peripheral individuals keep to the outside. (See figure 3-1). This spatial arrangement, however, is far from formal, and the chart is meant only as a generalized construct. At any moment, any rider "has the right" to situate himself anywhere he wants or, more to the point, anywhere he can. Whereas peripheral space is uncontested, access to the center depends on sheer power. Typically a khan, his chapandaz, and whatever other supporters will advance into the melee as a unit: chapandaz first

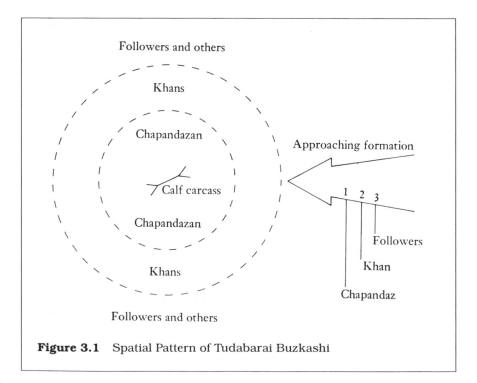

Figure 3.1   Spatial Pattern of Tudabarai Buzkashi

THE TUDABARAI PRIZE. A successful chapandaz accepts his cash prize at the end of a dispute-free play cycle. The white-bearded town crier readies his praise chant at left.

with khan close behind and sundry supporters in tow. When progress towards the center gets really rough, the chapandaz urges his horse forward and the khan whips it hard on the rump. Only the strongest horses and riders ever come near the calf on the ground.

Action is most turbulent when the carcass still lies underfoot at the start of each play cycle. Horses rear forward and buffet one another as their riders wait for a momentary chance to grab it from the ground. This initial struggle lasts from a few seconds to ten minutes or more. Its intensity depends primarily on the prize offered by the tooi sponsorship. Each of the 40 or so play cycles entails its own prize or *salem*. These are determined by the tooi-bashi, who dispenses funds entrusted to him by the tooi-wala. At the start of each play cycle, the tooi-bashi specifies the new prize, its kind and its amount. Today these are normally in cash and vary from 50 to—in extreme instances—2,000 or 3,000 afghanis. Prizes in the past took more symbolic forms, and even today a tooi-bashi may offer a turban cloth, a silk cloak, or a rifle from time to time. From cycle to cycle he varies the prize values and so can orchestrate a kind of rhythm throughout the tooi. The longer the struggle continues, furthermore, with the calf carcass still on the ground in a given play cycle, the higher the tooi-bashi raises the prize.

The actual communication of prize amounts is far too raucous an activity for any self-controlled khan to perform. This full-throated task falls instead to the *jorchi* or "town crier," who takes his cues from the tooi-bashi and then shouts the prize amounts over the heads of the struggling horsemen. The jorchi himself is perhaps the single person least involved in the continuous struggle for reputation. As "town crier" (a status he may or may not actually hold in everyday life), he exists at the disposal of anyone who pays for his services. Only a person of, in effect, hopelessly low status would allow himself to be so blatant in the flattery of others. Here he broadcasts the salem increments specified by the tooi-bashi:

> 100 afghanis . . . 100 afghanis . . . oh chapandazan, who will take it? . . . 100 afghanis . . . lift it . . . now 200 afghanis . . . who will take it? . . . ride oh ride . . . oh chapandazan . . .

and so forth until the carcass is finally lifted from the ground and one or more of the chapandazan begin to break through the mass of other horsemen.

When the carcass is finally off the ground, the chapandaz—or chapandazan—in control push through the mass towards its periphery. Other horsemen try to wrest the calf away, and often it falls to the ground without "free and clear" mastery having been demonstrated. Eventually, however, something like the required degree of control is attained by one rider, and the play cycle moves towards completion. The successful chapandaz drops the carcass in splendid isolation, rides a short distance away from the newly forming mass, and is accompanied there by a number of other horsemen: his khan (his horseowner/employer), the tooi-bashi, the town crier, and whoever else chooses to pause before joining the next play cycle.

Here several transactions occur. Typically, they start with the salem presentation by the tooi-bashi to the chapandaz. The prize is permanently his, although he may give it to a friend or even to his khan for safekeeping during the game. Next the khan usually follows with a bonus of his own, which matches or even exceeds the salem prize. Thus the chapandaz receives two prestations in addition to whatever the khan already pays him as a salary. The town crier may comment informally as these awards occur. At their completion his delivery becomes more stylized, and he bellows an impromptu chant in praise of the winners: the horse, the chapandaz, but most notably the khan on behalf of whom man and beast have triumphed:

> O, the horse of Hajji Ali,
> On him rode Ahmad Gul.
> How well he ran,
> How skillfully he took it,
> How he took it away,
> How he showed what he is,
> How the name of Hajji Ali rose,

> How we all hear his name,
> How his pride is complete.

And:

> O, the horse of Hajji Sheerin,
> With Sar Khel on his back.
> He leapt like a deer;
> He watched like a leopard.
> I stared at the horse
> And shouted its worth:
> "It's now worth one lakh."[4]
> "Oh no," said Hajji,
> "It's worth much, much more."
> We must honor Hajji
> Lest the snow start to fall
> And the town crier starve.
> All those who do not honor his name—
> May God impose a punishment upon them.

Half humorous, half serious, and with no honor of his own to maintain, the town crier is free to broadcast the reputation of others. In return, he is usually tipped a small amount of money by the khan whose name he has praised. A really sizable tip may prompt an encore.

Meanwhile, the concentric mass of horses and men has formed again where the calf was last dropped to the ground. Yet another play cycle starts. It can last from less than a minute to more than half an hour and stretch in any direction across the steppe. No formal limits exist in time or space. In six hours or so of play, the cycle may recur 30, 40, or 50 times. Halfway through the day, the calf carcass has already been torn into a ragged shred of skin, bone, and gristle. The last play cycle before its retirement is contested with special zeal, and the salem prize usually features the mangled remains themselves: monetarily worthless, but redolent of sanguinary pride. A brief pause marks the introduction of a new carcass. Otherwise, play continues nonstop. For the khans and their chapandazan, each cycle offers fresh opportunity for the demonstration of power and the enhancement of name.

For the tooi-wala as represented by his tooi-bashi, the opportunity—and conversely, the risk—comes in the continuous flow of events, all day, every day. His control of the situation is tested in two ways: economically as one prize after another must be disbursed with each play cycle, and politically as different interpretations of play threaten dispute and disruption. Ultimately, both the buzkashi and its sponsorship will be evaluated for three qualities: the number of participants (the more the better), the size of the prizes (the bigger the better), and the degree of control (the tighter the better). It is a tricky combination. The third seeks to limit competition to that activity which is unequivocally understood as play. Control depends on cooperation, and the sponsorship task is to keep these two ethics, the competitive and the cooperative, balanced and in separate perspective. Not enough competition makes the play dull. Insufficient cooperation renders the tooi chaotic. Dull play usually reflects a small-scale enterprise which, because it is soon forgotten, does its sponsorship no good, but little harm. Chaos is more vividly remembered. In the absence of cooperation, the frame wherein men contest buzkashi can shift from play to combat in a flash of physical abandon. Events in the first-order game quickly escalate to struggles on higher orders, and the locus of authority is suddenly foregrounded.

This potential for explosion is enhanced by the catch inherent in tudabarai buzkashi. With no spatial demarcations anywhere on the field, the question repeatedly arises: How free is free and how clear is clear? Obviously, the possibilities for dispute are endless. Since, as they say, "the calf has four legs," more than one chapandaz can grab hold at once. When it falls to the ground, the issue turns on who, if anyone, had sole control. One man may claim to have taken the calf from another at the last moment. Late in a game the shredded carcass may even be torn in two. Was the score, in the Moslem parlance adopted by buzkashi, *hallal* ("proper") or *haram* ("improper")?

The spatial structure of a tudabarai dispute features the same concentric pattern that has characterized play. Now, however, the

ON THE WAY TO A SCORE. Whip clenched between his teeth, a chapandaz breaks loose from the melee, but—the ever-present question—can he take the calf truly free and clear?

chapandazan often withdraw from the center to be replaced by the khans themselves. What follows is an instance of the second-order game in which contestants struggle for authority over each other in the dispute context. Naturally, it is not recognized as a "game" by those involved. They are too busy shouting and screaming at a minimum, perhaps flailing their whips, or even brandishing newly drawn knives. Now the buzkashi itself has "become a buzkashi."

Supposedly, the tooi-bashi is vested with adjudicative authority over play. He, in principle, decides hallal from haram and communicates this decision to the jorchi town crier. His success in this critical role depends on several factors. One, of course, is the extent of uncertainty in the particular play cycle itself. Most cycles are virtually indisputable in their outcomes, but inevitably some entail close calls. A second consideration has to do with the political relationship between khans with rival buzkashi claims. Men who are otherwise allies hesitate to offend one another; real-life opponents, on the other hand, can ill afford not to be aggressive even in what normatively is understood as a game. Finally, these buzkashi play disputes—their number and their seriousness—are a reflection of the tooi-bashi himself and, ultimately, of the authority that he derives from the tooi-wala. The more this sponsorship has a name for authority over its qaum, the less contentious the entire process. Weakness, however, encourages challengers in the competition for control. Powerful or weak, the tooi-bashi has only name—his own and that of the tooi-wala—as a resource in his umpire role. No formal body of official personnel backstops his decisions. Mounted on horseback like other men, he wears no special dress and blows no whistle. From event to event, the degree to which his authority is recognized may vary considerably.

The ideal tooi-bashi matches fairness with firmness, but in tudabarai disputes this combination is difficult to maintain. With the salem prize to be awarded, a tooi-bashi has three options. He can make no award at all, but this course is hardly consistent with the desired sponsorship impression of openhanded hospitality, and represents an admission that the cherished play ethic has been seriously interrupted. Second, he can divide the prize between the two rival claimants or even duplicate it so that both receive full measure. To do so is undoubtably fair but sometimes implies a lack of firmness. Soon, participants speculate, the tooi-bashi will have to bribe everyone on hand to keep the peace. Duplicate awards, furthermore, stretch financial resources that may already be thin. Third, he can opt for firmness and declare a sole recipient for the prize. Here fairness takes a backseat, at least temporarily, so that the locus of tooi authority may remain secure.

This last option is the most commonly employed, at least at the outset of a dispute, but its consequences can lead to even more disruption. Over the course of a buzkashi, the prudent tooi-bashi will try to balance questionable calls between rival khan factions, but each play cycle has its own sense of immediacy. To recall Habib, "Once it starts, nothing else matters." The tooi-bashi and those who wish him well try to temper this singlemindedness by emphasizing the playful frame: "It's only a game; we play for the fun of it; we're all friends here; it doesn't matter." These wishful sentiments are reiterated throughout every tooi, but they often fail to forestall the excitability of a Habib.

Usually, some sort of reconciliation is effected. Otherwise, no tooi could survive for long. The rival khans accede, with varying degrees of graciousness, to whatever settlement has been formulated, pacify the bellicose inclinations of their respective entourages, and resume their original demeanors of men concerned merely with innocuous shouq interest. To the extent that the settlement has been imposed by the tooi-bashi, the locus of authority remains with the festival sponsorship. If, however, the main peacemaker has been someone unassociated with the sponsorship, his reputation, rather than that of the tooi-bashi and the tooi-wala, will have benefited, and the issue of tooi authority will have been thrown in doubt.

Occasionally, reconciliation does not occur at all. The differences in interpretation are too wide; the political relationships between the rival factions are too hostile; the tooi sponsorship is too weak, and no one else can successfully fill the vacuum. Then one of two developments typically occurs: either there is an outright fight, or those who are least reconciled leave the tooi.

Of these two possibilities, leaving the tooi is by far the more common. Fighting may take place, but it tends to be spontaneous, isolated, and quickly ended or at least deescalated to the level of sullenness. It is seldom that two khan factions actually do pitched battle in a buzkashi encounter. One, generally the one from further away geographically, is inevitably the weaker, and all participants (despite normative protestations of undifferentiated camaraderie) are intimately aware of which faction has more men in the field. For the weaker faction to fight in any deliberate fashion would thus be foolishly self-destructive. On the other hand, what prestige remains must still be salvaged. Rather than staying, therefore, under circumstances perceived as unfair and thus demeaning, the weaker faction—a khan or an aggregation of khans and whatever entourages—turns its collective back on the tooi and rides away.

Although the variations are infinite and dependent upon particular circumstances, there are, in general, two interpretations of such departures. Each, in effect, places blame, embarrassment, and subsequent loss of prestige on a different set of participants. Those who leave are usually in an oppositional relationship to those at the center of tooi support, and it is these two factions who cast aspersions on each other. Tooi supporters typically call the departed faction cowardly; they are men who cannot hold their own, who had already done poorly in actual play, who run when difficulties arise. The unreconciled faction, on the other hand, calls the tooi supporters inept; they are men who should never have presumed to sponsor a tooi, who do not know how such things work, who cannot control their own undertaking.

It is this last allegation that implies the most political damage. For the tooi-wala and his supporters, their enterprise has succeeded through a series of ever more challenging events only to fail in the final arena. Success in this most public phase of the tooi brings rewards in prestige far greater than those available in the earlier gatherings. By the same token, however, failure here is all the more widely observed and remembered.

If the tooi survives these risks, it continues for as many days as were announced on the invitation. In the daytime, virtually all male participants, save the tooi-wala and some of his household servants, gather in one great throng at the buzkashi field. They disperse in the late afternoons towards their separate mehmandar guest houses, where the long winter nights are spent in various activities. In instances where the tooi-wala has really great resources, he may organize some large-scale evening extravaganza, such as wrestling or the quasi-salacious dancing of pubescent boys. Usually, however, nocturnal activities are structured in terms of individual guest houses where all those present—mehmandars, khans, and entourage members—indulge in that universal pastime of Afghan life, conversation.

It is in these conversations that events of the buzkashi day are first reviewed: as events of pure play, but also more or less consciously as the stuff of politics. Both the play cycles and whatever disputes arose from them are remembered and interpreted in exhaustive detail. What a great horse is that bay of Mir Akbar Khan! How it can stand still over the calf and not be moved by the others! It's all in the chestbone: the way it points forward, not down. That horse . . . when it was young, Mir Akbar Khan had them raise its feed trough, and that's why its neck is so long, why it rises above all the others. What a horse! Did you see the way its chapandaz, Qorban from Qala-i-Zol, took that last calf this afternoon? That Qorban reminds me of the great Haq Mohammed, chapandaz many years ago for Wakil Abdul Latif, who could grab the calf with either hand and hang by one foot in the stirrup. And what about that dispute between the Cheragh Uzbeks and the Omar Khel Pushtuns? Some say that Uzbek chapandaz had a rope up his sleeve and tied the calf to his saddle horn. It was a bad row. Could the tooi-bashi handle another one like it? How much prize money do you think is left? Will the tooi last the full three days?

From time to time in these post-game gatherings, buzkashi talk turns frankly political: No, Hajji Ramatullah is obviously not what he once was. His qaum is smaller than when he controlled all the canals above Angor Bagh. You could see it today in that dispute his people had with the Ferghanachis. Three years ago I helped him with that mess over the bridewealth. You remember? When Sayyed Ali Khan got so angry at him? I stood by him then, but now. . . .

At the end of the final afternoon, the last play cycle is contested with special zeal. Whoever's horse and rider win the last calf or *akherulaq* (lit., "last goat" in Turkmani and Uzbeki) gains special renown. In presenting this prize, the tooi-bashi—or even the tooi-wala, who perhaps is finally in attendance—may take a last initiative in the form of a farewell speech. Already, however, some guests have begun to drift away. A few may go by the tooi-khana to pay their respects, but the party is suddenly over. The ad hoc qaum of tooi supporters—mehmandars, khesh members, closest followers—ceases to exist in any active sense. The tooi-wala and a few old friends gather in his guest house for self-congratulatory post mortems: reveling if the tooi went well, telling themselves it went well even if it did not (and remarking dismissively that "it was only a game"). Still to come in most cases is the actual rite of passage, but circumcisions, and especially marriages, are better arranged by women. For the men, the tooi has meant buzkashi, and finally—for better or worse—the buzkashi is done.

AFTERMATH

Events in the aftermath of a tooi are difficult to specify. The guests disperse: some to other khan compounds, some to town. Most go home, where even in leisurely winter certain affairs demand attention. Meanwhile, who knows, word may have come of another tooi, and members of the buzkashi khan elite begin the whole process all over again.

Otherwise, however, the aftermath is nebulous: far less well-defined than either the step-by-step preparations or the spectacular festivities. It takes the form of reflections, both private and shared, but in any event quite random in their occurrence. Their impression-istic content is similar to that of the nocturnal talk in tooi guest houses. Each khan, in fact each individual of whatever status, has taken his own impressions home with him and will apply them, con-sciously or unconsciously, to his own participation in the fourth-order game of mundane politics. For the tooi-wala sponsor, the stuff of these remembrances is particularly crucial in his own geographi-cal area. Here at home he has tried to foster an image on the basis of which followers, both old and new, will acknowledge his authority. Further afield, authority is less an issue, at least for the moment, than simple fame. And yet who knows what will transpire in an unknowable future? All khans have to start somewhere, and who knows how wide their authority may someday spread? Even in guest houses far removed from the tooi, an aura grows around the names of Hajji Aulia and Wakil Ishaq Khan. They are men with reputation and, by extension, with e'tibar political credit provided by impressions which in turn derive from events. "Everyone knows them," and not least of all because of the buzkashi tooi.

TWO TOOIS—SUCCESS AND FAILURE

Kunduz Province, where most of the fieldwork for this study took place, is both more economically developed and more ethnically diverse than many other sectors in the North. Until this century its central area consisted of malarial swamp, and the saying was, "If you seek death, go to Kunduz." In the 1920s, however, initiatives were taken to drain the land whose fertility then proved unparalleled. "If you seek gold, go to Kunduz" is the modern axiom. Today Kunduz constitutes a socially transitional area: still predominantly rural but less traditionally based than any of the other provinces from Badakhshan to Faryab. As an element of Kunduz culture, the buzkashi tooi tends to be less well preserved and less politically important than elsewhere. It retains, however, its essential elements, and Kunduz khans still sponsor toois every winter. Two of these serve to exemplify the institution in success and failure.

The first tooi took place the winter before I arrived in the field. Obviously, my lack of firsthand observation poses a problem in analysis. In terms, however, of impressions—the critical factor in any such activity—the tooi was later remembered so vividly by so many informants that it provides an ideal aftermath example of what a successful tooi should be.

From start to finish, the tooi-wala and his closest associates exercised full sponsorship authority. As the eldest males in a family that dominated the political life of a large and ethnically homogeneous village, the tooi-wala and the tooi-bashi were brothers. Like most families in the province, theirs had immigrated from elsewhere in Afghanistan less than a century ago. The village, however, had grown under family patronage, and the father of the two brothers had been a representative to the National Assembly a generation earlier. A hajji, like his father before him, the tooi-wala had gone to Mecca at the relatively young age of 34 and had served as a favorably remembered mirab water master some years afterwards. His brother was the village arbab and thus mediated relationships between the villagers and nearby government officials. Together the brothers owned much of the best watered land near the village. Together they had planned the tooi for three years.

This fraternal cooperation was fundamental in the eventual success of the tooi. The tooi-wala readily admitted as much and, indeed, boasted of the bond. It had been, he said, his brother who had first dreamed of the tooi, invested his own money, used his own contacts, written the invitations with his mosque-acquired education, and been the best of all possible tooi-bashis.

The tooi-wala also proudly acknowledged the general support of his qaum. Here his usage of the term was broadly inclusive and encompassed not only his agnatic kin, but also everyone else who supported the tooi. His khesh kindred came mostly from the home village. His mehmandar subsidiary hosts, however, came from a significantly wider geographical range and included not only fellow Uzbeks, but also Pushtuns and Hazaras. They totalled a remarkable 120 and had consented to serve, said the tooi-wala, for two reasons: he had done the same for their toois in the past, and his family had always been known as "servants of the qaum." Presumably, he and his brother now deemed it time to draw on this store of political credit.

That they were able to do so is evident from the recollections of many informants. The tooi-wala himself loved to talk about his enterprise, and never was his memory more vivid than when he volunteered an individual-by-individual account of guest/host pairings; off the top of his head, he listed 79 guests (of whom 70 bore honorific titles such as khan, hajji, wakil, and arbab) and their 49 hosts. Perhaps his memory was helped by the fact, a "fact" at least in his mind, that all these pairings had been decided by him in advance and dictated to the mehmandars, who agreed without argument. As for the festivities themselves, "The whole country," he said, "was there: ten or twenty thousand people, and every house from here to Kunduz had to be used as more and more came." These included, he added, "not only 90 percent of those I invited but also carloads of strangers from all over Afghanistan." It was a "six-province tooi with men from Badakhshan, Takhar, Kunduz, Baghlan, Samangan, and Balkh."

Other informants, even those unallied with the tooi-wala politically, tended to corroborate: "Now my father is gone and my own beard is white, but never have I known such a tooi." Questions about numbers led to instant hyperbole. How many horsemen were on the field? "Five thousand . . . no, ten . . . no, fifteen. Mir Sayyed Khan told me that he had to ride an hour and a half to the east to find a private place to pee." The shenak gifts had totalled, according to the tooi-wala, 146,000 afghanis, so the salem prizes could be correspondingly high. In the words of one chapandaz,

> They were all high: a thousand, fifteen hundred, two thousand each time. The money was in his hand (of the tooi-bashi), not in his pocket. Once when the calf was on the ground, the salem got to 3,700 afghanis, and we chapandazan had to ask that it be reduced for fear one of us would die in trying to grab it. Ghafour (who had since emerged as one of the leading chapandazan in

Kunduz) changed horses five or six times and still never even saw
the calf.

Most noteworthy of all was the extent of authority that the sponsorship exercised. The tooi-wala and his tooi-bashi brother followed "the
traditions of our father and grandfathers." They recruited four other
khans, each representative of a different ethnic constituency, who sta-
tioned themselves in separate quarters of the buzkashi field and
helped keep the peace. Other informants marveled at the control. "It
was all done by discipline," said one, "by cooperation of the qaum." In
the words of another, "When the field was cleared for the horse race (an
event sometimes staged at really large toois as a break from buzkashi),
I said to myself, 'The police must be here: Men in uniforms from town.
Which of us khans in turbans could clear away such a crowd?'"

The tooi-wala himself, however, never went near the buzkashi
field. Secure in the authority exercised faithfully by his brother, he
maintained the demeanor of perfect host at home in the tooi-khana.
No distant arrival was too late to find an unruffled welcome. The
total impression was one of systematic control in which events took
place according to prediction. Guests came as they were invited to
come and stayed where they were assigned to stay. The buzkashi
lasted for all of its announced three days and suffered no cataclys-
mic disputes. Qaum support proved both wide and solid. The tooi
served both as an expression of that support in the present and as
an enhancement of it for the future. A year after the tooi, the name of
its sponsor and, to lesser extents, the names of his closest associates
were still mentioned whenever conversation turned to buzkashi. It is
impossible, of course, to tell just how far the effects of his tooi
reached into the fourth-order game of politics, but undoubtedly it
contributed to the great reputation he enjoyed for political authority.
As the successful sponsor of the best attended, most competitive,
and most strictly controlled social event of the year, the tooi-wala
had realized the hope that his name would rise.

The second tooi occurred in February, 1977, in circumstances conducive to very detailed observation. The tooi-bashi was my close friend
and a man of considerable worldliness. This latter quality enabled him
to conceptualize abstract patterns in quite a helpful way. Unfortunately
for the tooi, his sophistication scarcely compensated for a lack of
qaum authority. This second tooi thus constitutes a more negative
example of buzkashi sponsorship. Without the necessary support, it
was virtually inevitable that things would go wrong from the start.

As in the first case, the tooi-wala was a prosperous landowner
and a hajji. There, however, the similarities ended. In the second
instance, significantly, the tooi-wala was a Pushtun rather than an
Uzbek. These two broad ethnic groupings are the most numerically
powerful in Kunduz Province. Uzbeks dominated the area from the

sixteenth to the nineteenth centuries. In the last hundred years, however, various Pushtun populations have moved into Kunduz, either voluntarily or at the forceful encouragement of the central government. Thanks to continued intervention of the government, itself Pushtun controlled since 1747, much of the choicest land has gone to these Pushtun immigrants with the Uzbeks being left with less fertile areas. As recently as the 1930s there were outbreaks of interethnic combat, and while the situation is less volatile today, political loyalties still fragment along this fundamental divide.

With their landholdings relatively guaranteed by the government, Pushtuns often settled without the usual concern for agnatic cohesion. Thus, the village of the tooi-wala was ethnically diverse. In the sense of residential unity, his aggregation of tooi supporters (his qaum) had less of a densely knit core. This problem was exacerbated by the fact that buzkashi in Kunduz is still primarily identified as an Uzbek pastime. For many of the Pushtun khans, buzkashi lacks traditional shouq interest, and the tooi-wala was that much less able to count on an ethnic base of assistance. Finally, he was in his late sixties and infirm. Impressions of forceful authority would have to come from someone else.

It was against this rather unpropitious background that the tooi preparations began. The first two steps seemed at the time to proceed smoothly, but the choice of the tooi-bashi would cause problems later. Here the tooi-wala decided to rely on his father's brother's son. The subsequent difficulties did not derive from the proverbially ambivalent nature of this relationship. In this instance, the tooi-bashi was 30 years younger than the tooi-wala and deferred to him in almost filial fashion. Rather, the tooi-bashi was also a chronic invalid and, however well liked in buzkashi circles even by the Uzbek khans, could hardly be the man to epitomize control.

The third step of the preparations took place without undue difficulty, and khesh support appeared sufficient. It was in the fourth step that the tooi first ran into public trouble. Without a qaum of fellow Pushtuns on whom to rely as the core of mehmandar hosts, the tooi sponsorship was left with the far more problematic help of local Uzbek khans. Sponsorship hopes had run high until this point: guests would come from as far away as Balkh; the tooi-bashi would compile the guest/host pairing arrangements in advance "to save all my mehmandar friends the trouble"; there would be one big buzkashi salem prize of 5,000 afghanis, "the greatest ever in Afghanistan."

These hopes were badly compromised when the mehmandars met. Of the 56 invited, only 33 arrived, and two-thirds of these were Uzbeks. Ethnic diversity would cause trouble all day. The common language of general discussion was Dari, which serves as a lingua franca throughout the North. Among themselves, however, Pushtuns spoke Pushtu and Uzbeks spoke Uzbeki.

Bad luck revealed the weakness of this tooi enterprise only moments before lunch. With the first two decisions (when to hold the tooi and for how many days) settled without too much dissension, a rider arrived with word of another tooi set for the same time. As can so quickly happen at any point in the tooi process, reconsideration was now necessary. Like the tooi at hand, this other one was scheduled to last three days, and much of the discussion turned on the matter of resources. How much of a qaum did this other tooi-wala have? Who would be his tooi-bashi? How many mehmandar hosts would help him? How much money would he have for salem prizes?

Lunch was held in abeyance by what constituted, ever more obviously with each minute of irresolution, a real threat to the tooi. Finally, an uneasy consensus was achieved and, because it was so uneasy, phrased in idioms of rationalization:

> Yes, of course, our tooi will be the better one; yes, of course, our tooi would attract more participants if they were held on the same dates; but, after all, it's only for fun anyway, and, after all, the other invitations were issued first; so, who cares, we can postpone our tooi a day or two for the sake of friendship.

The ceremonial meal at midday had its hoped-for effects: a commensal decrease in tension among the mehmandar recruits and a full-bellied sense of good-neighborliness towards their tooi-wala host. Contention soon developed, however, over the two most reputation-oriented decisions: whom to invite as guests, and how to pair guests with hosts. Bit by bit, the atmosphere shifted from agreeable to argumentative. Voices rose, and arms waved. Neither tooi-wala nor tooi-bashi was personally able to command authority. In effect, they all but abdicated control and relied instead on the help of two or three more influential khans. The mehmandar session ended with a semblance of consensus, but when everyone had shaken hands and left the tooi-khana, the mood of its residents was far from ebullient. The sheet of guest/host pairings which the tooi-bashi had so confidently prepared in advance now lay discarded behind an empty teapot. Too few hosts had come in the first place, and as one man remarked ruefully, "everyone present had had his own idea." In the course of a confused three hours, two dozen proposed guests had gotten lost in the shuffle and now had no hosts at all. The tooi-wala somewhat dubiously said that he could absorb some of them. Others had to be scratched from the list completely.

The actual tooi festivities started as scheduled. These coincided, however, with the last day of the other tooi, and the relatively poor attendance (certainly far less than the 90 percent claimed in the previous example) was blamed on the competition: Surely all the others would come the next day. By noontime, the shenak gift total was a meager 16,300 afghanis. Now it would be difficult to provide even acceptably-sized salem prizes for three days of buzkashi play. No further mention was made of the unprecedented, but now clearly impossible, 5,000 afghani single salem.

One problem led to another. Not only did many of the invitees not come, but some of those who did arrive were less than cooperatively disposed. A spectacular dispute erupted in the tooi-khana compound at the end of the first day's buzkashi. A perceived insult in the fourth-order game of local politics had recently turned a particularly prestigious guest/host relationship into one of virulent (if temporary) opposition. Now neither khan wanted any part of the other, and the guest had nowhere else to go. The tooi-bashi failed to reconcile the situation, lost his temper, and angrily tossed the shenak money of the guest back in his lap. With infinite disdain, the guest slowly brushed the bills onto the ground and got to his feet. Now, he said, the tooi sponsorship itself had refused his kindness and withdrawn its hospitality. He would leave the money on the ground, abandon the tooi to its sure disintegration, and go. As he gathered his entourage around him, other individuals tried to mediate, but by now the breach was too great. The guest left in high dudgeon and took with him two agnatic relatives also recognized as khans, several unrelated khan friends, two chapandazan, and a number of personal retainers. When I saw him three days later, his first concern was whether (as he hoped) the tooi had collapsed because of his departure.

It was on the buzkashi field, however, that the lack of sponsorship authority was most publicly observable. Despite a brave effort, the invalid tooi-bashi could not ride horseback for more than an hour at a time. As such, he had to find someone to whom to delegate an authority that had never been great in the first place. The ethnic division between Pushtuns and Uzbeks made it pointless to select a single khan from either grouping. The one man who might have managed was, ironically, the guest who had gone home in disgust. Thus, the sponsorship settled on a solution that proved disastrous. It transferred the adjudication role of the tooi-bashi to, of all people, the jorchi town crier.

The decision was not without a sort of crazy logic. As a member of neither major qaum, the town crier, for one thing, was essentially nonpartisan. As a singularly low-status Jugi, furthermore, his exercise of the tooi-bashi role could hardly be construed as a threat to the true occupant of that status. Now the tooi sponsorship foregrounded the normative frame of fun: "It's only a game, after all, and we're all friends here. Let the town crier decide hallal and haram. He can be a joke tooi-bashi."

Unfortunately for the sponsorship, this fun frame proved ephemeral. However nonpartisan and subordinate to the true tooi-bashi, the town crier lacked even the most minimal of names. Time and again, disputes quickly got beyond his control. "Hallal or haram?"

The judgment of the town crier was more and more open to challenge with every play cycle.

The critical moment came halfway through Day Two, when the real tooi-bashi, well enough for the moment to sit on a horse, raised the prize in one of the especially valuable play cycles that punctuate the more routine flow of buzkashi activity. He had been criticized for his low prize offers—50 and 100 afghanis—and now responded with the announcement of a 1,000-afghani prize. For the past several hours the quality of play had been a bit dull and almost halfhearted, but now the struggle turned intense. Dust rose in great clouds. Men shouted, and horses whinnied. Still the calf carcass lay on the ground. The tooi-bashi raised the stakes even further with the addition of traditional prize items: first a cloak and then a turban cloth.

Suddenly the buzkashi came alive, with all the chapandazan in the melee and all of their khans behind them. The calf was lifted and dropped repeatedly with no one man in "free and clear" control. Finally, however, the whole mass moved 50 yards or so across the field as several riders lunged and dragged and struggled over the carcass. When it fell this time, no fewer than four chapandazan claimed to have had sole possession. These were quickly supported and, in fact, supplanted by their khans, each one of whom besieged the tooi-bashi for recognition of success. The town crier was immediately jostled aside and wisely rode his swaybacked pony towards the periphery. The tooi-bashi called for quiet, but by now his voice was lost in the din of controversy. All pretenses of authority collapsed completely.

The chaos continued for fully ten minutes as the khans and their retinues came face to face in the mayhem. A few blows were half struck, but physical conflict was mostly confined to pushing and shoving. No one dismounted. Each khan whose chapandaz was involved now attempted to dominate the middle of what was still a concentric mass. As each tried to press his own claim, other khans also drove their horses towards the center. Hitherto held in abeyance by the normative buzkashi frame of play, real-world political factions were suddenly activated. Bit by bit, the uproar became dominated by a few individuals. None of these, as it happened, had had a horse and rider directly involved in the disputed play cycle. Rather, these dominant khans now supported the claims of lesser men politically affiliated with them. Two of the four rival claimants were men with relatively small qaums, and the dispute centered instead on the two other more important factions.

Of course, not everyone on the field was an active participant. Even the two opposed factions consisted of various individuals whose commitments were variously conceived. Other men, especially low-status followers of khans who themselves were relatively inactive, stayed to the outside. All, however, paid close attention to what had become a political microcosm.

The two factions were structured in essentially residential terms. One, the more numerous, derived from a locality close to the actual tooi. The other faction, while still quite powerful, was smaller and had its roots in another province. Finally, the tooi-bashi enunciated the inevitable: the horse and rider whose khan was associated with the more numerous faction had taken the calf and deserved the salem prize.

The town crier was summarily called back to announce what apparently had now been decided once and for all. As he started his praise chant, however, the khan who had lost the decision declared that he would leave the tooi and take his faction with him. Too numerically weak to stand a chance in actual man-to-man combat, they chose the only other honorable option: withdraw their support from the tooi and ride away in ostentatious contempt. Immediately, several would-be mediators attempted to intervene: men with feet in both camps whose own names would rise if their reconciliation efforts succeeded. The tooi-bashi was more than ever in a bind. On the one hand, he needed to placate the unhappy faction to keep the tooi intact. On the other, as a khan and as the tooi-bashi of a buzkashi still scheduled to run for another day and a half, he dared not appear too weakly irresolute. With his sponsorship resources—human and material—already strained, he could only hope for the best of a bad situation.

He decided that the least costly move entailed the duplication of salem prizes. While this practice may be regarded as magnanimity at some toois whose sponsorship is obviously well endowed from shenak gifts and other sources, here the illusion of graciousness was all too transparently a cover for appeasement. The departing faction, even more humiliatingly for the tooi-bashi, now had to be talked into returning. All told, this one play cycle cost the sponsorship 2,000 afghanis, two cloaks, and two turban cloths.

More than material wealth had been lost. In a mercilessly public arena of volatile events, the tooi-bashi had had decisions forced on him by the behavior of other individuals. As such, he and the sponsorship which he represented had suffered enormously, both in the second-order game of control over play disputes and, by extension, in the third-order game of control over the tooi as a whole. To make matters worse, more material resources than the sponsorship could afford had now been expended, with less than ever left for subsequent prizes. In an attempt to regain the initiative, the tooi-bashi asserted himself in the very next play cycle. Seizing upon a particularly spectacular chapandaz exploit, he voluntarily, and with apparent spontaneity, awarded another expensive prize (500 afghanis), as if to state that authority and resources were still intact.

No one was particularly impressed. While no other critically serious disputes occurred that second afternoon, the locus of tooi authority remained very much in the balance. Over supper in the tooi-khana, there was much worried discussion about what to do on the third day to come. As an experienced informant once observed, "It's on the last day of a tooi that the real truth starts to show." With much already lost, the decision was sensible if woefully belated: the tooi-bashi role would now be shared by the two most prominent khans at the tooi, a Pushtun and an Uzbek. These men were honest with respect to salem prize funds, fair when balanced in tandem, and authoritative over their two respective ethnic constituencies. The trouble was that neither man was particularly close to the sponsorship in terms of real-life ties. Had they been recruited prior to the tooi, appearances of solid support probably could have been fostered. As it was, however, the transfer of authority was self-evidently remedial.

As a strategy for conflict management, it did, however, work the next day. Differences of opinion still took place, but these were never allowed to become full-blown disputes. The prizes were as sizable as the sponsorship could still afford, but a lack of real incentive kept the level of play almost perfunctory. By noon, several informants spoke of boredom. The original tooi-bashi resumed his role, only to stop play two hours early. He was concerned, he announced, that everyone have time to start towards home. Others remarked sotto voce that his real worries were with too little salem money and too much dispute potential: better to end the tooi with at least some semblance of authority preserved.

Many horsemen had already started to drift away. Some had even left a day early. Back at the tooi-khana afterwards, the mood was subdued. Physical health had become an authentic concern for both the tooi-wala and the tooi-bashi over the past ten days. Now, in the late afternoon, they sat with their closest associates and said little. Everyone seemed aware that the tooi had fallen far short of expectations. This realization was made all the more painful by reports that the other tooi had been a reasonable success. Finally, one man tried to make the best of it. "Well," he summarized without much conviction, "it was only a game, you know, and the really important thing to remember is that no one got hurt."

Once again, it is impossible to measure precisely the effects of this tooi on the fourth-order game of real-life politics. Once again, the tooi and all that happened in it are part of a larger process of impression management in which the appearance of authority is an important factor in its reality. If the effects of this particular tooi could somehow be isolated, they would probably approach a neutral balance: from the standpoint of the sponsorship, neither very helpful nor very harmful. To be sure, the tooi ran its announced time, but in a manner badly controlled and ultimately lackluster. In contrast to the enthusiastic quality of recollections about the successful tooi, aftermath talk in this case dwindled almost at once. A month or so later, no one volunteered the topic, and the more persistent of my inquiries were met with patient boredom. The only informant to elaborate with any warmth was the khan who had gotten angry and left the first afternoon:

> Now you know what happens. It's been only a month and who talks about the tooi? Who mentions his [the tooi-wala's] name? It goes to show that he didn't know how to handle a tooi. Why do you think I left? You told me afterwards that the tooi continued for its full three days. Three days of what? Now you know. You should have left with me and saved your time.

No real-life political disaster befell the tooi-wala immediately, nor, other informants yawned, would it necessarily do so in the future. Old friends and close followers of the tooi-wala would quite likely stick by him, or at least not desert because of the tooi alone. His day-to-day authority would probably stay about the same as it had been. The principal loss would come on the less obvious level of potential for initiative: Now the world had a fairly clear sense that he could achieve only so much and no more. The attraction of new allies and supporters would prove that much more difficult. On the whole, the tooi settled in the popular mind, not as a debacle, but as a mediocrity. Its only real winners were the two khans who had been appointed in desperation as last-day tooi-bashis.

One other event in this second tooi prefaces the next chapter. At mid-morning on the first day of festivities, word arrived at the tooi-khana that the subgovernor of the administrative district in which the tooi was taking place had levied an ad hoc tax on the activity. Immediately the tooi-wala and two of his most influential townsmen friends left by car to talk with the official. They returned two hours later and 5,000 afghanis poorer. The subgovernor, they said, had demanded that the money be contributed to the building of a mosque with which his patron, the provincial governor, had gotten himself identified. The tooi-wala had little choice: either the money would be paid or the tooi would be cancelled, by a force of uniformed soldiers if necessary.[5]

This confrontation introduces a second—and vertical—axis of buzkashi politics. Whereas the interactions described in this chapter have occurred horizontally among the khans, the increasingly significant struggle for authority all over Afghanistan now is waged between two different modes of political organization: that of the local khans and that of the national government. Toois in the past took place without any suggestion of government intervention. Now the traditional autonomy of the buzkashi tooi is threatened. Even more remarkable is what the government has done to the game itself.

NOTES

[1]Barnes, J. A., "Networks and Political Process," in *Social Networks in Urban Situations*, ed. J. Clyde Mitchell (Manchester: Manchester University Press, 1969), p. 69.

[2]In some of the larger and more prestigious toois, play is vaguely oriented near a man-made earthen mound where nonhorsemen sit as spectators. These typically include rich merchants from town, government officials on sufficiently good terms with the khans to attend in safety, and other males too old, sick, tired, or poor to be on horseback.

[3]While most chapandazan are relatively low-status clients of their khans, a few of those now active in Kunduz Province are themselves the scions of powerful families. They proudly accept salem prizes (on which they are not economically dependent) but do not enter into typical chapandaz contracts with khans. Such exceptions to the rule of chapandaz as client have probably always existed. They may be on the increase, however, as the traditional structure of patron-client relationships is diluted. Thanks to their prominence in government-sponsored buzkashi (see chapter 4), the status of chapandazan as a category is gradually being enhanced.

[4]One hundred thousand [afghanis].

[5]In a subsequent interview the subprovincial official described the event in rather different—and very normative—terms. Yes, he had heard of the tooi and had been interested in it (as, indeed, he was interested in all things that occurred in his subprovince). Yes, he had mentioned this interest, but the tooi-wala and his friends had come mostly on their own accord. They had come, indeed, to invite him to the tooi, and it was unfortunate that his duties precluded attendance. His would-be host would no doubt have spent much money in his honor had attendance been possible. The official then suggested that such expenditure be made instead to the mosque, and the tooi-wala willingly agreed.

4

BUZKASHI IN PROVINCIAL TOWN AND CAPITAL CITY

These old khans from the countryside, you know, they watch me all the time for the slightest sign of weakness. I must always make it clear to them what sort of man I am.

—Abdul Khaleq Rafiqi, Governor of Kunduz
(personal interview, April 30, 1977)

The leader of our country, the Hon. Mohammed Daoud, President of the Republic, yesterday afternoon witnessed the buzkashi matches which took place in Ghazi Stadium between teams from the northern areas of the country. Thousands of patriotic and republican-minded persons welcomed the founder of the republic with spontaneous enthusiasm.

—*Anis* (government daily newspaper, October 24, 1977)

In 1953 the national government of Afghanistan resolved to bring buzkashi across the Hindu Kush to Kabul. The man most influential in this decision was Mohammed Daoud, then in the first year of his autocratic decade as Prime Minister (1953–1963), and later to assume ultimate, if short-lived, authority as President (1973–1978). At that time, however, the titular khan of Afghanistan was its king, Mohammed Zahir, on whose birthday the Kabul buzkashi would be played for the next 20 years. With his fall at the hands of Daoud in 1973, the tournament continued for another five years under republican auspices. After Daoud himself was killed in the revolution of April, 1978, the new Marxist regime (of Noor Mohammed Taraki) managed to present its own version of national buzkashi in October. Now two other coups have followed in rapid succession, nearly 100,000 Russian troops are embroiled in a bloody war, and still the government of Afghanistan (under Hafizullah Amin in 1979 and Babrak Karmal in 1980) goes to the considerable difficulty of staging Kabul buzkashi.

Since its inception a generation ago, government sponsored buzkashi has gradually been established not only in Kabul, but also in northern provincial centers. First entrusted with this task by the monarchy, the Afghan National Olympic Committee (ANOC) has continued, through successive regimes, to develop a buzkashi infrastructure with a special bureaucracy in Kabul and governor-directed organizations in each of ten northern provinces. In ordinary times, the ANOC has at its disposal infinitely more resources than even the greatest of local-scale khans, and the buzkashis it sponsors possess, for the most part, an inexorable quality of authority on display.

Once again, it is a matter of frames: What is it that's going on here? Most informants would answer, "Just a game," or perhaps with reference to the new qarajai form, "a sport." With infinite subtlety, however, that other, less frivolous, and more political frame is available and, indeed, imposes itself on whatever level of consciousness. The observations of Abner Cohen describe exactly this aspect of government buzkashi:

> . . . although a regime may come into office and maintain itself for some time by sheer force, its stability and continuity are achieved mainly through the symbolism of authority which it manipulates. Subjects do not start their lives every morning examining the dispositions of power in their society to see whether the regime is still backed by the same amount of force as before, or whether the force has diminished and the regime can therefore be overthrown. The stability and continuity of the regime are made possible by a complex system of symbolism that gives it legitimacy by representing it ultimately as a "natural" part of the universe.[1]

Here is the vertical axis of impressionistic politics in government buzkashi. To be sure, khans still compete horizontally among each other for the glory of having a successful horse and rider, but the real focus of competition now moves to a bigger league between the two modes of political organization: the khans and the government.

In ordinary times when the government possesses at least some semblance of legitimacy, this "competition" appears anything but problematic. Very, very seldom is government authority overtly challenged in one of its own buzkashis. Such events serve more as affirmations of that authority, and those who participate have no illusions about who is ultimately boss. Political life, however, is never so simply an issue of either/or. Rather, the "for real" frame question at a government buzkashi is phrased in terms of extent: how much control is the government organization able to exercise? As events of the late 1970s suggest, that question is hardly idle in Afghanistan, where apparently placid experience can suddenly turn volatile.

With regard to buzkashi, the government "symbolism of authority" has been represented through a pervasive routinization of otherwise volatile events. More than any tooi-wala khan on the local level, this new, and infinitely more resourceful, sponsorship has been able to control the metaphorically uncontrollable. Analytically, this development takes place on two levels: the switch in buzkashi forms from tudabarai to qarajai, and the standardization of time, space, and participants. The transition to qarajai with its well-defined boundaries, cumulative scores, team identities, and authorized umpires is objectively real to everyone, and buzkashi men often comment on its comparative ease of adjudicative control. Less readily identified per se are the effects of standardization across the whole scope of buzkashi experience, but these subtleties—like those of frame—are all the more powerful for their indirection.

This chapter treats government buzkashi in three sections. The first describes its provincial level as expressed in Kunduz during the 1976–1977 winter season. The second provides a month-and-a-half case study of Kunduz buzkashi events as they revolved around the provincial governor. The third shifts to Kabul for a summary account of the national tournament.

Buzkashi in Provincial Centers

The preparations for government buzkashi in the provinces can be quite elaborate, but—unlike the case at a tooi—their outcome is far from problematic. This contrast is handily exemplified by a brief interlude from the second tooi described in chapter 3. In the midst of the mehmandar recruitment session at the sponsor compound, an unarmed soldier in bedraggled uniform walked into the courtyard. The discussion had reached the critical point of which guest would stay with which host, and tempers flared on all sides. The tooi-wala, however, abruptly left the hubbub, heard what the soldier had to say, and returned to announce, during a lull in the commotion, that there would be a government buzkashi in Kunduz town the following Friday. The soldier continued on his rounds to other khan compounds. At the tooi-khana there was little or no subsequent mention of the news. It had been received in the sense of a command: on the next Friday virtually every khan who had been notified was on hand with horse and chapandaz.

This undisputed compliance came, of course, in recognition of government authority based on government resources: ultimately, an army full of soldiers with loaded guns. On the provincial level, this power is embodied by the *walis* or "governors." Appointed directly by the head of state, these officials function as near autonomous satraps. For the most part they are Pushtuns alien to the North, but many take an active interest in government buzkashi; it can relieve the monotony of an afternoon far from Kabul, and, perhaps more to the point, some heads of state (Daoud, for example) have been known to favor its development. As the personification of government at one of its provincial buzkashis, the wali governor is analogous to the tooi-wala sponsor. All that happens there reflects on him and, through him, on the government.

His tooi-bashi analogue is a local khan who bears the title *rais* or "president" of buzkashi. This status originated with the start of government buzkashi a generation ago. In ANOC theory, the *rais-i-buzkashi* is selected by his fellow khans, but a keenly interested wali may make the choice himself. The nominee must then be approved by the Olympic Committee and finally by the Minister of Defense who, under the Daoud administration at least, was also honorary chairman of all buzkashi in Afghanistan. This process is itself intensely political as rival khan aspirants compete for government favor.

While his position is unsalaried and essentially honorific, the rais-i-buzkashi is responsible to the wali for the promotion of government buzkashi: for the presentation of provincial matches and for the development of a provincial team. Responsible to him in turn are the *ma'aweneen* (sg. *ma'awen*) or "deputies," each of whom represents a subprovince. It is these men who deal directly with their fellow khans for the provision of horses and chapandazan upon which provincial buzkashi remains dependent. The rais-i-buzkashi president is expected to foot the bill for incidentals: calf carcasses when no other donor materializes, the public address system that constitutes an important new communicative resource, refreshment for the wali and his entourage, soft drinks for the chapandazan (who prefer Fanta to Coca-Cola), and sometimes even the cloaks and turban cloths that serve as their salem prizes.

His only reward is prestige: "to be called 'rais sahib, rais sahib, oh rais sahib' everywhere he goes." Sometimes this emphasis on reputation reflects direct access to the centers of government power. In Kunduz during 1977, the rais considered himself always welcome at the home of his patron the wali. He was commonly believed, furthermore, to be personally known to President Daoud, who once a year shook his hand at the Kabul tournament. He could, in the words of one informant, "walk in the door of the Presidential office without the permission of anyone." In reality, he almost certainly could not have done so, but the mere belief enhanced his name.

Various other functionaries contribute to the buzkashi effort. The army commandant deploys a company or so of soldiers to promote order. The town mayor usually coordinates labor for stadium maintenance. In the 1976–1977 season the provincial second-in-command or *mustufy* frequently presented the chapandazan prizes. All told, there may be a hundred or more men involved in the presentation of a buzkashi.

To continue the tooi analogue, this group constitutes a government qaum for the wali sponsor. Its support, however, is now far more dependable. Whereas support for the tooi-wala consists of an egocentric and impermanent "action-set," government organization exists already in corporate form. Its application to provincial buzkashi can often be quite haphazard, with various officials in Friday afternoon roles unassociated with their workweek functions. Even so, this makeshift cast represents the means for achievement of a new predictability.

All the wali need do, in effect, is say the word. It is disseminated from official to official and implemented without question. The khans of whichever subprovinces will field teams in the next buzkashi are notified. Each must produce his horse and his chapandaz. No remuneration is offered. If the wali is known to take a serious interest, however, the khans almost always comply. Not to do so would risk his displeasure, whether immediate or delayed. Some khans speak resentfully of fines for no-shows. Resentful or not, no one doubts that the wali can impose his own arbitrary will in such instances. This initial compulsion foreshadows a significant, if subtly accomplished, theme in government buzkashi: the reduction of khan authority and their removal to the periphery of events.

RECOGNITION AT A GOVERNMENT BUZKASHI. On February 14, 1977, the governor of Kunduz successfully assumed authority over a traditional buzkashi. Here he and Western-dressed subordinates applaud a score.

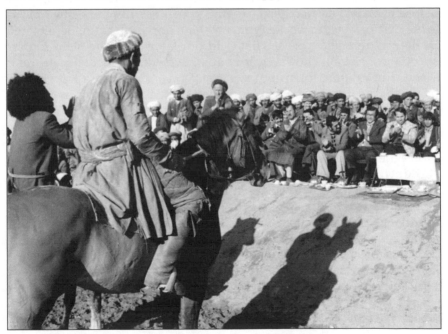

Government buzkashis are usually organized for days of public ritual, for the most part religious: Fridays on a more or less regular basis, and holidays such as Eid-ul-Fitr and Eid-ul-Qorban when their lunar cycle dates fall within the buzkashi season. Depending on which dates are relevant to which regimes, some government buzkashi occasions may be overtly political. In February, 1977, for instance, the twin events of constitutional ratification and presidential election were marked by buzkashis in several provinces. Whatever the occasion, however, it is the wali whose decision authorizes play.

When they go to a government buzkashi, khans may still have their retinues, but these tend now to be smaller and less motivated by concern for self-defense since, ordinarily, no violence occurs outside the first-order game. Upon arrival in town, khans from the countryside often head for privately owned, urban compounds called *seraiha* (sg. *serai*) and spend several hours in conversation with other visitors. These serai compounds are named for their owners (that is, serai-i-Hajji Nazukmir or serai-i-Abdullah Khan) and may serve as factional headquarters for khans from the hinterland. Meanwhile news of the buzkashi has traveled by word of mouth through the town bazaar. In Kunduz it is sometimes announced in the center square by a public address system, which otherwise blares Radio Kabul hour after hour. Soon the crowd begins to stream towards the buzkashi ground that lies beyond a cemetery at the edge of town.

Whereas the site of tooi play is often not decided until shortly before it starts, all northern provincial centers have specified areas for use from week to week. Typically their precise location is dictated by natural terrain: a broad, flat field of play with some elevation for spectators. Usually, however, humans have enhanced the scene, and a sense of cultural plan imposes itself on nature. Of all provincial buzkashi facilities in the North, by far the best equipped is in Kunduz, where a natural amphitheater is crowned by several concrete structures (See figure 4-1). These represent the administrative units of government organization: the dominant Kunduz town pavilion in the middle, and the smaller (and generally neglected) camps of the subprovinces to either side.[2] Below them stretches the field of play with its qarajai circles and flags. It is vaguely bounded on two sides by inclines where the spectators sit. A third side sometimes has the semblance of a boundary line in chalk. The fourth fades indefinitely towards a cluster of trees in the distance.

Within the central Kunduz pavilion, space is likewise delineated far more precisely than at any tooi (See figure 4-2). Here architectural forms approach the neatly geometric, and access to the various sections is strictly controlled. In the middle, spaially as well as structurally, sits the wali, and to either side are his special guests and

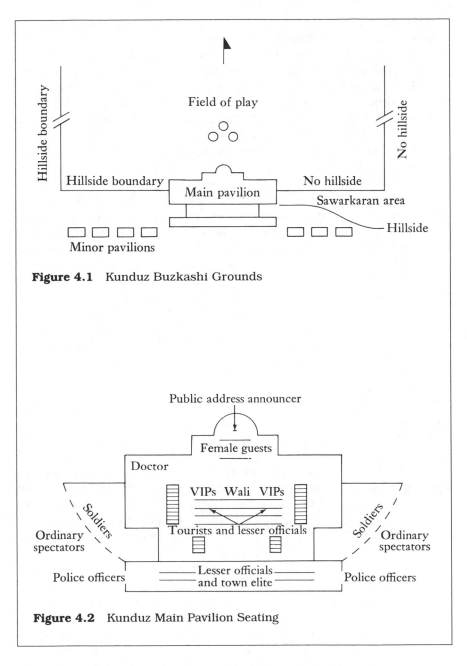

Figure 4.1 Kunduz Buzkashi Grounds

Figure 4.2 Kunduz Main Pavilion Seating

senior associates in the provincial government. Minor guests (including perhaps a sprinkling of foreign tourists and lower officials) sit behind him, while below him on a concrete apron are several rows of women: the family of the wali and their female friends from town who have abandoned the veil for the head scarf of the new urban elite. Also on the apron are a white-coated doctor (reputed by skeptics to be no more than a wali sycophant who favored his patron with periodic rubdowns) and the announcer with a public address system directed at the pavilion. Guarding access to the government pavilion are uniformed soldiers and police officers. Within the pavilion virtually everyone wears Western dress. Beyond it on the slopes to either side are the thousands, sometimes tens of thousands, of ordinary men and boys in turbans and robes. Among this undistinguished throng sit many of the khans who now find themselves relegated to the sidelines of what traditionally has been their game. At the very top of the main pavilion looms a large black and white photograph of the Afghan head of state. Seldom venturing far from Kabul, even in relatively peaceful times, he is still less frequently present in person at a provincial buzkashi.[3] Symbolically, however, his intended position is clear. In 1976–1977 the face of Mohammed Daoud was both beneficent and forceful as it surveyed the scene: the ultimate tooi-wala, whose sponsorship the wali merely personified.

The buzkashi is scheduled to start at a set time, usually 2:00 P.M., and thus after the midday prayer. As the hour approaches soldiers, policemen, and the announcer combine in attempts to clear the field. Invariably, a crowd of kibitzers on foot, horseback, or even bicycle try to heft the calf carcass, but these are shooed away. The rais-i-buzkashi delegates someone to implant the far flag around which the play will turn. Meanwhile the two teams of chapandazan don their special uniforms. The boots and the telpak caps remain from tooi buzkashi, but now the trousers and tunics have been sewn in town from imported corduroy. On this level of subprovincial competition, not all the uniforms match, but it is usually clear at a glance which chapandaz goes with which team.

Five minutes or so before the appointed hour, a mass of horsemen congregate in formation at the far flag (see figure 4-3). As they face the main pavilion, the rais is mounted in front and flanked by his two subprovincial ma'awen deputies. Their teams of chapandazan stand side-by-side in a line behind them, and still further back comes everyone else who has a horse at the buzkashi: the *sawarkaran* or "horsemen." The town crier, now outlandishly attired in an antique Turkman hat, cavorts more clownlike than ever in and out of the several rows.

Now everyone waits in place for the arrival of the wali. He may already be on hand, in which case the buzkashi can start. Otherwise,

Figure 4.3   Initial Formation for Provincial Buzkashi

play is deferred indefinitely, and sometimes an hour or more will pass with all in readiness, but no wali. Patience may be strained, but neither horsemen nor spectators dare protest.

Finally the wali makes his appearance, shakes hands with his entourage, and acknowledges whatever applause the announcer can generate. As he takes his seat, the horsemen start to parade inwards towards the pavilion, while a tape recorder plays martial music over the public address system. Then the announcer begins his afternoon-long narration with a politicized welcome, such as was delivered in Kunduz on Friday, February 18, 1977:

> Honored spectators, greetings to you all. We hope that you welcome the spring after a winter of snow. This grand and dignified buzkashi which you are watching today is being held on the occasion of the election of the first President of the Republic of Afghanistan, Mohammed Daoud, loyal son and founder of the nation. In order to witness the contest, the Honorable Mr. Rafiqi, Governor of Kunduz, directors of the government administraion, and thousands of spectators are present at the stadium. Now the chapandazan and sawarkaran are slowly approaching the pavilion for the official presentation. The chapandazan and sawarkaran are accompanied by Mr. Mirabuldin Khan, president of buzkashi for Kunduz province, and Mr. Abdullah Kakar, his deputy general. The horsemen are slowly approaching for the official presentation. They are now ready for the official presentation. At the signal of the buzkashi team president the official presentation has been made. I hope the spectators will applaud the chapanda-

zan. The president of buzkashi has now congratulated the governor on his attendance, on the new constitution of Afghanistan, and on the election of the President of the Republic, Mohammed Daoud the Great, loyal son and founder of Afghanistan. The Governor welcomed and accepted those words. Now the buzkashi competition in honor of the first constitution and president of Afghanistan has started.

The "official presentation" consists of a mass bow by all the horsemen towards the wali. Then the rais blows his whistle, and the neat formation explodes in a blur of movement. The chapandazan gather in a ragged circle around the calf and may, indeed, start struggling over it without further notice. The sawarkaran horsemen whirl and dash towards the sideline. There they are meant to stay until play ends. Some of them may be powerful khans, but the qarajai rule applies as much to them as to their lowliest clients: Only the chapandazan now "have the right." The sole permissible function of the non-contestant sawarkaran is to keep substitute horses in readiness for the actual players.

Meanwhile the first-order game of buzkashi begins. With only the two teams of chapandaz in contention, play is faster and more free-wheeling than at a tooi. The calf carcass is quickly grabbed from the ground. Long gallops carry it around the far flag and back towards the scoring circles. Now the premium is on deft technique rather than sheer power. The urban-based spectators in the central pavilion clap polite appreciation from neat rows of padded chairs. The thousands of anonymous onlookers sprawled on the earthen slope to either side respond less stereotypically. Most are essentially passive. To be sure, these men have come of their own accord to watch a spectacle unmatched for physical excitement in the life of provincial towns, but now they sit in subdued detachment. Occasionally some display of chapandaz agility evokes a round of muted applause. Mounted but idle on the sideline, the sawarkaran fidget.

In theory, play is confined to spatial boundaries marked on the field. In practice, however, the chapandazan pay little heed to the bottom of a hillside or a blurred white line. Sometimes they stampede into the ordinary spectators, who scatter while the rais-i-buzkashi blows his whistle and the announcer shouts, "*Out ast!*"[4] Then play lurches to a halt, and the calf carcass is somewhat haphazardly returned to fair territory. Likewise, the sawarkaran horsemen are prone to trespass onto the field of play. Contrary to qarajai rules, they sometimes deliver substitute mounts to wherever the action is, and even join it for a moment or two before the rais orders them back.

As with space, so with time: supposedly standardized but in practice quite casual. Now play is divided into two halves. These and the halftime interval are formally established at the outset. Typically however, time is kept by the ordinary wristwatch of the wali or some-one in his retinue, and a minute or two more or less is hardly noticed. Even more to the point, the wali can always extend the play or call a halt at will.

To do so—or, indeed, to effect his wishes in any respect—the wali need hardly bestir himself. The rais-i-buzkashi is always at his dis-posal. So too is the announcer, whose public address apparatus enables one voice to dominate the environment far more forcefully than is ever possible in the traditional context. For the 1976–1977 Kunduz season the announcer served in mundane life as provincial district attorney: a fast talker and an ambitious client of the wali. His afternoon-long monologue always conveyed the same message of gov-ernment authority over the game. Its range, however, was limited. Rigged for temporary use and aimed primarily at the pavilion audi-ence, the public address system failed to reach most ordinary spec-tators and could barely be heard on the field.

The ease of adjudication in qarajai buzkashi means that scores occur without dispute in most instances. Authority in the matter is meant to reside with the rais-i-buzkashi, at whose signal the stylized process of score recognition begins. When a calf is dropped in the appropriate circle, play ceases and four riders approach the main pavilion: the rais, the successful chapandaz, the deputy of that team, and the town crier. What transpires then takes no more than a minute or so, but in its brevity is contained a dramatization of the new buzkashi relationships.

The rais shouts out the name of the chapandaz and his horse-owner khan. The announcer repeats the name of the chapandaz, pro-vides an update of the team score, and sometimes—but not always—includes the name of the khan. This latter omission derives from mere inadvertency. As a bureaucrat from Kabul, the announcer is oblivious to the whole rural world of reputational politics. For him, the khans quite literally have no names. At the mention of his name over the public address system, the chapandaz rises in his stirrups and bows towards the wali. From the mass of ordinary spectators, meanwhile, the horseowner khan walks onto the concrete apron and presents the traditional bonus to his rider. It is his sole moment of recognition. The town crier launches into his tooi-style praise chant on behalf of the khan, but the message is often overwhelmed by some new comment from the announcer. The khan goes back to his seat. The riders, acknowledged perhaps by a nod from the wali, return to the game, which may already have begun again without them.

The dominance of the wali, the performance of the chapandazan, and the redundancy of the khans—all three themes are even more pronounced at the end of the afternoon. When play finishes in Kun-duz, the sawarkaran stream back onto the field and mix once more with the chapandazan. Now all the horsemen crowd around the side of the concrete apron. The women who have sat through the buzkashi immediately beneath the wali are quickly escorted to a convoy of cars under police protection. Their places are taken on the apron by participants in the final awards ceremony: those chapandazan who have scored points, the rais, the two subprovincial team deputies, and whoever the wali delegates to give away the awards. Invariably a top-level member of his provincial administration, this individual in 1976–1977 was most often his second-in-command mustufy. For the wali to leave his seat and present the awards himself would be vaguely undignified in a culture where authority is often symbolized by the lack of a need to bestir oneself. The wali sits still and speaks softly in the apparently effortless assurance that others will do his will.

One by one as their names are announced, the chapandazan come forward. The rais-i-buzkashi has their prizes ready, but this final tooi-bashi presentational role is too important at a government buzkashi to be left to an old-line khan. Rather, it goes to the Western-dressed mustufy who takes the prizes from the rais—a cloak, perhaps, to each chapandaz who dropped the calf for a two-point score, and a turban cloth for each man who merely rounded the flag—drapes them over their recipients, and embraces the chapandazan on behalf of the wali. The khans are more than ever lost in the crowd. Their traditional voice, the jorchi town crier, has fulfilled his pathetic qarajai role as equestrian fool and ridden away.

All attention ultimately focuses instead on the wali. It is under his sponsorship that the buzkashi has taken place and its performers are now rewarded. In this sense, the chapandazan now exist almost as his clients. The wali may interrupt the awards process at any time to call this or that chapandaz to his side. He may even take advantage of what constitutes his largest weekly audience to make a few extemporaneous remarks on whatever topic. Usually, however, the Kunduz governor contented himself with a set of cheers to which the prudent responded on cue. These cheers are phrased on an impromptu basis:

Wali: The leader of the revolution, may he live!
Spectators: May he live!
Wali: Afghanistan, may it live!
Spectators: May it live!
Wali: The tricolored flag of Afghanistan, may it live!
Spectators: May it live!
Wali: The champion army of Afghanistan, may it live!
Spectators: May it live!
Wali: The friends of Afghanistan, may they live!
Spectators: May they live!
Wali: The enemies of Afghanistan, may they die!
Spectators: May they die!

Finally the wali turns to leave. No one else in the central pavilion has moved. With retinue in tow and flanked by soldiers with fixed bayonets, he walks unhurriedly to a black limousine. It is in this brief interval that decisions about the next buzkashi may be dictated to his rais. What for a tooi requires several problematic rounds of hospitality and discussion can be the work of a moment for the wali. A police-car siren wails. All other traffic has been blocked. The convoy departs in a cloud of dust that settles over the faces of khans and other now undisputably lesser men.

In the aftermath of a Kunduz government buzkashi, the wali usually returns to his guarded compound in town. A few wealthy men will have driven their own cars, and these too bump from pothole to pothole towards the main bazaar. Most spectators walk the mile and a half to the serai compounds, the tea houses, the cinema, or whatever late afternoon destination awaits them. Rickety buses range from the four corners of town towards more remote villages. In the course of this general dispersal, topics of talk are infinitely varied, but much of it deals with the day's buzkashi. Unlike the evening guest house conversations at a tooi, however, the names of the khans are hardly mentioned. Only real aficionados speak of these traditional patrons.

Nor is there much attention paid to the matter of which team won. The whole concept of team play is too new to make much sense. For the most part cooperation between chapandazan teammates has been minimal, and the subprovincial team identities seem little more than conveniences. The real winner is the government as embodied by its tooi-wala analogue, the wali. It has been a subtle triumph realized, in fact, most fully when least noticeable. To the extent that the entire process has been represented as a predictable routine with competition confined to the first-order game—to that extent the government has gained in the realm of impressionistic politics and thus in authority. It is not, at least analytically, the sort of victory which can ever be absolute. Disputes, while infrequent, do sometimes arise. Even in their absence, the fundamental dimensions of experience can never be entirely standardized: boundary lines on the field are still trespassed; times for the start and finish of play still prove only approximate; sawarkaran still stray into the action contrary to stated rules. Provincial buzkashi thus represents a middle step in the routinization process between the problematic tooi of the countryside and the predictable tournament of Kabul. This intermediate quality was dramatically illustrated by a sequence of Kunduz buzkashis early in 1977.

A KUNDUZ SEASON

Unusually deep midwinter snows covered the steppe from December onwards and made buzkashi play all but impossible. By the time these finally melted, a number of would-be sponsors had started to formulate plans. Horsemen travelled the muddy rounds from compound to compound with rumors of prospective toois. Some were actually held; others never materialized. In town, meanwhile, a more certain set of buzkashi initiatives was underway. From mid-February through the first week in April, games were played on the government field with enough regularity so that, at least in retrospect, a kind of sequence presented itself. Week after week of buzkashi events unfolded like a serial with plot, moral, and cast of characters. The lead role, even when he was physically absent, was played by the Kunduz wali: a wealthy Pushtun from Kandahar, far south of the Hindu Kush, with two master's degrees from foreign universities, a gigantic if generally good-natured ego, close (and ultimately fatal) ties to President Daoud, and a lively interest in buzkashi. Abdul Khaleq Rafiqi also became my all-purpose patron whose support, however whimsical, provided me with research carte blanche in the province for as long as he remained governor. Even so, I could never quite tell, at least from his words, what really motivated his enthusiasm for buzkashi. "It's good for the people," he used to tell me with the blandest of smiles. "It gets them together, you know, and gives them some fun."

This sequence of wali-oriented buzkashis ran for seven weeks:

February 13–14	Privately sponsored tooi in Chardara sub-province in which the wali intrudes
February 18	Government sponsored game in Kunduz town with the wali in charge
February 25	Government sponsored games in Kunduz town with the wali absent and his mustufy in charge
March 4	Government sponsored game in Kunduz town with both the wali and the mustufy absent and the commandant in charge
March 11	No government sponsored game; wali absent
March 18	Government sponsored game in Kunduz town with the wali in charge
March 25–April 4	Interprovincial tournament in Kunduz town with the wali and the ANOC vice-president in charge

Most of this late season activity did, indeed, amount to "fun." From moment to moment, the locus of authority was usually so well-defined as not to be an issue in any conscious sense. Three times, however, serious disputes erupted with a sudden shift in frames.

The first such encounter occurred at a private tooi held outside Chardara, some twenty miles of rutted dirt track west of Kunduz. As the first buzkashi event in more than a month, the tooi attracted most powerful khans from the nearby valleys. Both the tooi-wala and his tooi-bashi were Uzbeks, but the area Pushtun population was also well represented. The first day passed without untoward event: inevitably, a few small disputes but no serious disruption. Much more remarkable was the news communicated by his client and fellow Pushtun, the rais-i-buzkashi, that the wali intended to come himself on the morrow.

Walis and other government officials are often invited as a matter of form to khan-sponsored toois, but they seldom actually go. With their urban backgrounds, few of them have an authentic shouq interest in buzkashi. Rather more pragmatically, such attendance entails the risks of entrance into a social arena where the writ of government authority runs with little consistency. For the tooi-wala there was, in any event, little option: Like it or not, he would have to make the wali welcome. Hopefully, from his perspective, the wali would behave merely as a passive spectator.

Such, however, was not to be the case, and the first concession of authority was made even before the wali arrived: a change of buzkashi venue from the open steppe to a field near the Chardara bazaar. The wali, so the rais said, had "suggested" the change. Throughout the morning of that second day, small disagreements developed between the rais and the tooi-bashi. Essentially it was a matter of which buzkashi to play: the tooi tudabarai or the government qarajai. Play stopped completely several times as the two men bickered. Uzbeks backed the tooi-bashi; Pushtuns the rais. The acrimony became so sharp that only the obligation to host the wali kept the tooi together.

It remained, in fact, for the wali himself to restore order on his arrival. This event was heralded shortly after noon by a truckload of uniformed soldiers complete with the carpets, tables, and chairs to construct a primitive semblance of the VIP section in the Kunduz pavilion. Half an hour later the wali appeared at the head of a five-car convoy full of friends and fellow officials, all in Western dress. The fitfully contested buzkashi ceased abruptly. Soldiers wielded riot sticks to clear a path to an earthen mound where the wali and his retinue would sit. After some rather sporadic applause had died, the wali made an impromptu speech about the new constitution drafted in Kabul. He shook hands with the tooi-wala and the tooi-bashi but never mentioned them or their sponsorship in his remarks.

Similarly, it was now the wali-backed rais who tended to assume authority over the actual buzkashi. The form of play was summarily decided by the two Pushtuns: qarajai with its spatial precision, but without potentially divisive teams. Only those dressed like chapandazan could play; all others had to stand in a line that would serve as one of the boundaries. None of the prominent Uzbeks had any voice in these decisions. The tooi-wala had effectively been reduced from all purpose sponsor/authority to mere provider of chapandazan prizes.

Now play proceeded with far fewer overt disputes. Conflict flared momentarily when an Uzbek chapandaz dropped the calf on the scoring circle. "Haram," cried the rais. "Hallal," shouted the Uzbeks. At a government game in Kunduz town, the rais decision would almost certainly have gone unchallenged, but his word by itself counted for little here. Even supported by the presence of the wali, the rais could not settle the matter by himself and had to appeal directly to his patron. By now, Uzbek leadership had been tactically vested in the Chardara deputy. Himself a part of the government buzkashi organization, this Uzbek khan, so the tooi sponsorship reasoned, could hardly be so arbitrarily dismissed by the wali.

The wali listened first to the Uzbek deputy and then to the Pushtun rais. His decision was instantaneous: "Haram," he said, "No score." Play resumed at once, but the wali had not finished. He ordered the deputy to dismount and to sit by his feet. Then in an infinitely quiet voice the wali made his points: that the rais, his rais, had the authority and that a deputy should naturally serve as a supporter. The interprovincial tournament would start in another few

KUNDUZ PROVINCIAL BUZKASHI, FEBRUARY 1977. A weary Habib receives congratulations (and yet another prize turban) from the *mustufy* (provincial second in command).

weeks, and what, the wali asked rhetorically, would people think if such disputes were allowed to happen then? With the least perceptible of nods towards his mustufy two chairs away, the wali wondered aloud what would happen if the finance department in Kunduz were allowed to run this way. When the deputy tried to respond, he was told to keep quiet, to look the other way, to watch the buzkashi. Finally the wali dismissed him with a word. The deputy remounted and rode back into the action, but a statement had been made. Only a very few other men had heard what the wali said. Everyone present, however, knew that a powerful khan had been humbled with apparent effortlessness. Lest anyone be confused about the new locus of authority, the wali went one final step further. A muted word sent one of his subordinates towards the parked cars. Moments later, the man returned and handed the wali a sawed-off shotgun, whose snubnosed barrel was shrouded in a green velvet cloth. With no fanfare whatsoever, the wali placed it on the table in front of him.

There it remained all afternoon, neither handled nor even mentioned but unquestionably real. Both a symbol of government power and an instrument of self-defense in case matters grew worse, the shotgun with its green cloth served as the perfect veiled threat.[5] There were no more disputes over rais decisions. The wali was all smiles as he assumed another sponsorship prerogative and congratulated the chapandaz who had won the final play cycle. It had been fun, the wali said, and everyone was invited to a government buzkashi in Kunduz town the following Friday. The soldiers waved their riot sticks, the convoy car doors slammed, and the wali disappeared as abruptly as he had come. In the compelling language of events, he had registered the really critical victory of this buzkashi: on his own behalf as an individual politician, on behalf of Kunduzi Pushtuns at the expense of their Uzbek rivals, and—most importantly—on behalf of the government organization at the expense of khan autonomy.

Four days later many of these same tooi participants were among the thousands gathered in Kunduz for the government buzkashi. February 18 happened to coincide with the confirmation of Daoud to the Presidency, and the announcer introduced the afternoon with the politicized speech already quoted. With the wali in watchful attendance, the whole affair passed without a hint of disruption. Emboldened, perhaps, by his intrusive dominance over the tooi, he somewhat whimsically halted an uneven match at halftime and entirely restructured the teams: one would be the Hawks and the other the Eagles and never mind whose chapandaz rode whose horse. This novelty proved somewhat confusing for several of the chapandazan, who persisted in dropping the calf carcass in the wrong circle, but play was undeniably more even and the wali was pleased. As for the khans, they had not been consulted in any way.

Still welcome to present their respective riders with bonuses, the members of this traditional elite were otherwise left in oblivion. As a final note, the wali authorized the announcement of an interprovincial tournament scheduled for Kunduz in late March. In the weeks to come, the prospect of this wider-scale event would hover over ordinary Friday buzkashis with public excitement and private apprehension. Yes, all agreed, it would be the greatest buzkashi tournament ever held in the North, but, some wondered to themselves, would the wali be able to handle it?

On Friday, February 25, another government buzkashi game was sponsored in Kunduz. This time no special occasion was commemorated, and the play itself was routinely uneventful. One critical element in the process was, however, absent: the wali had gone to Kabul to keep abreast of rapid developments in national politics. In his place as the personification of sponsorship sat the mustufy, while the rais was now entrusted with the presentation of prizes. The absence of the wali caused no serious problems, but one all-but-imperceptible development foreshadowed the extreme difficulties which would arise a week later. Now the sawarkaran were considerably less tractable behind their boundary line. Several ventured onto the field to provide substitute mounts for the chapandazan and braved the verbal wrath of the announcer. Without the wali there to back him, his words had noticeably less effect.

The government game of Friday, March 4, promised once more to be essentially routine: an intraprovincial match between teams from the two administrative districts of Khanabad and Qala-i-Zol. Once more, however, the wali was elsewhere; a family funeral had called him to Kandahar. Nor was the mustufy available, and so the sponsor role fell to the third-ranking provincial government official, the military commandant or *commandan*. An amiable and elderly man, he would retire later in the year and was not especially known for qualities of forcefulness.

Two disputes early in the game proved too much for the rais-i-buzkashi to settle on the field and had to be referred to the commandan. Despite this sense of contentiousness, the match proceeded and Khanabad slowly pulled ahead. At this point, however, a pair of chapandazan, especially favored by the absent wali but normally unaffiliated with either team, swaggered to the main pavilion and announced that they would play for Qala-i-Zol. Ever anxious to please his wali patron, who would certainly hear about it, the rais agreed to this irregular proposal. Several Khanabad players complained, first to the rais and then to the commandan, but without effect. Finally, the entire Khanabad team resorted to the traditional tooi rejoinder to perceived injustice: they rode to the sidelines and refused to play.

Now left unopposed, several Qala-i-Zol chapandazan started to dump the calf in their circle and thus to score at will. The Khanabad team turned its collective back. Worst of all from the standpoint of government sponsorship, the thousands of ordinary spectators started to snigger. The carefully orchestrated spectacle was being made into a mockery.

The commandan could scarcely hide his fury and frustration. At first he tried to redeem the situation from his seat with the rais-i-buzkashi acting as go-between. A khan of great stature in the area, the rais was now observed scurrying back and forth in a most undignified style, and some of the sniggers turned to guffaws. The Khanabad chapandazan remained adamant; some even started to ride away. All semblance of government authority was going fast.

Suddenly the commandan abandoned his pretense of composure. Livid with anger, he ran from his seat and grabbed the public address microphone. "Dismount!" he screamed, "Dismount!" As the government security forces (soldiers and police) gathered, the Khanabad players had no choice but to obey. In what amounts in equestrian culture to a grudgingly shameful acknowledgement of superior power, the chapandazan got off their horses one by one.

Further degradation followed. "You care for no one but yourselves," the commandan shrieked through the microphone and then—far more to the point—"You have shamed the government which has provided this show." Now in a frantic rage, the commandan ordered the entire team imprisoned. Already unhorsed, the Khanabad chapandazan then had to walk in their clumsy boots all the way across the field and in front of the crowd to where a police detachment waited in commandeered taxis. Finally in control, the commandan ordered an ad hoc "Kunduz" team formed to compete with Qala-i-Zol, and play resumed, however haphazardly. Most spectators were far more interested in the progress of the Khanabad team towards prison in what amounted, analytically, to an extraordinary event in the third-order game for authority over the afternoon as a whole.

To be sure, the government had "won," and its authority had been publicly demonstrated. That the encounter had occurred at all, however, suggested that challenges were still within the realm of possibility. What had happened once could happen again, and who knew what the next outcome would be? On the level of impression management, the predictable had been rendered a shade more problematic. No government game was played in Kunduz the following Friday, March 11. For a third week in succession, the wali was otherwise occupied, and the notion of a buzkashi without him to control it was now quite unthinkable.

Instead, the sequence of buzkashis resumed on Friday, March 18, with the wali very much front and center. The approach of the intraprovincial tournament, now only a week away, made it all the more imperative that the impression of unquestioned authority be reaffirmed. Participants arrived to find the main pavilion more spatially inaccessible than ever. The concrete apron had been fortified so that no irate horseman could possibly ride onto it, and an earthen embankment now appeared between the VIPs and ordinary spectators. "Today," the wali told the announcer, "I want time kept to the second." Security personnel added to the increased sense of systematized control: a dozen mounted policemen with specially extended whips and a squad of soldiers at the central pavilion with rifles and electric prods. Not surprisingly, all excitement that afternoon was confined to the first-order game. No disputes flared. No noncontestants strayed onto the field. At the close of play, the wali took it upon himself to select the Kunduz tournament team unilaterally. No khans were consulted in the choice of their own chapandazan. By his own admission, albeit private, the wali had no time for such democratic niceties. The first full-scale interprovincial tournament ever held in the North was about to start, and with Kunduz selected as the host site, the wali was determined to establish himself as its tooi-wala.

In fact, the tournament sponsorship was somewhat imprecisely divided between Kunduz Province and the Afghan National Olympic Committee. Kunduz (under its wali) would host all visitors and provide play facilities. The ANOC (with a vice-president in charge of its seven-man contingent) would be responsible for the actual play. This arrangement was, however, loosely contrived at best and failed to specify who would be in overall command. Now that his control, phrased at least in the symbolic idiom of buzkashi, was demonstrably supreme over the khans of Kunduz, the wali was ambitious to extend it even further.

No interprovincial tournament on such a grand scale had ever been organized outside Kabul. Three other provinces (Takhar, Baghlan, and Samangan) would send teams to compete with the one from Kunduz in a round robin scheduled to last eleven days. Each afternoon would feature two games run according to ANOC regulations. That performance matched prediction in these fundamental respects was itself an accomplishment which enhanced, however subliminally, the impression of government authority. In the games themselves, disputes were few and readily settled in most instances by the ANOC officials. Now more than ever before in provincial buzkashi, the field was neatly bounded, the time accurately kept, and the nonfirst-order game players relegated to the sidelines.

No difficulties arose for the first few days. Gradually, however, the non-Kunduz contingents began to grumble that the wali was taking unfair advantage: that he could substitute horses indefinitely from nearby pastures; that he allowed his announcer to lead cheers

AN UNCERTAIN MOMENT. Habib (center) and Khol Mohammed (right) during the dispute of April 3, 1977 between Kunduz and Takhar. Other riders attend to the argument off camera.

for the home team; and that he used his role of host to influence the ANOC officials. Complaints increased with visitor frustration as the Kunduz team went undefeated day after day. The wali, in short, was considered by many to be attempting to rule a process that was both playful (and thus normatively independent of politics) and interprovincial (and thus beyond the proper scope of his jurisdiction). In just the same way that the Chardara tooi represented a downward intrusion in political scale on his part, so the interprovincial tournament entailed a politically upward presumption.

On April 3, the tenth day of the tournament, this resentment came to a head, and all appearances of fun and friendship were abruptly shattered. Previously unbeaten Kunduz trailed second-place Takhar in what had become the championship match. With the score 5–2 a few minutes before halftime, a Takhar chapandaz dropped the calf directly on the scoring circle line. Here again, the question was hallal or haram. The ANOC umpire on the field ruled in favor of Takhar, only to be overridden on a Kunduz appeal to his superior, the committee vice-president. True to the form of tooi protest, the Takhar chapandazan rode towards the sidelines while a Kunduz player carried the calf for an uncontested three points. When the ANOC field umpire tore off his armbands of office in disgust, the announcer cried with ill-disguised glee that the score was now tied at 5–5. All the allegations of unfair meddling by the Kunduz wali were being confirmed by events.

Such treatment was too shameful for the Takhar provincial rais-i-buzkashi to bear. With his team behind him, he rode to where his provincial supporters (khans and others) were seated. "Men of Takhar," he said, "let us go!" More than a hundred men rose to their feet and with their chapandazan followed the rais across the field towards a tented camp which served as Takhar headquarters.

The scene behind them had suddenly become extremely confused. Left without any opposition, the Kunduz chapandazan milled indecisively over the calf carcass. The tens of thousands of spectators who had crowded on the hillsides were abuzz with excitement. At the main pavilion worried officials rushed up and down the concrete stairs. In the midst of all this uncertainty the wali kept his seat and looked faintly bored. Unsure of himself so far from Kabul, the ANOC vice-president now rushed to where the wali sat, conferred with him briefly, and only then took the microphone: "Friends from Takhar, return at once. You must return. If not, Kunduz wins by default, and your team will be banned from the Kabul tournament next fall. Friends from Takhar, you have ten minutes."

By this time the Takhar contingent had reached its tented camp and would not budge. Now the great throng of spectators grew increasingly animated. Kunduz partisans began to clap in taunting unison as the ten minutes were counted down over the public address system. Partisan or not, thousands of people were now engrossed in the spectacle of a government enterprise gone very wrong. In the face of such public embarrassment, who would do what about it?

For all his apparent composure, the wali had a serious problem. From the start he had tried to cast himself in the role of unilateral tooi-wala of the tournament. Now, however, the whole affair had turned into a shambles at its most critical point. In vain he sent a subordinate to phone his counterpart in Takhar for the authority to use force, but word came back that the Takhar wali was unavailable. Without such authorization, the Kunduz wali clearly could not threaten "guests" from another province with imprisonment. Nor did the ANOC buzkashi sanctions seem to have any effect. The ten-minute deadline passed with no hint of compliance from the Takhar tents. None of the spectators seemed at all inclined to leave. Quite to the contrary, here was an event much more compelling than the first-order buzkashi game: Here was the real thing.

Finally the wali sent his mustufy assistant to the Takhar camp. This official had served in Takhar recently and could, hopefully, mediate. By now, all sides of the dispute were worried that word of it would reach Kabul. What would the Minister of the Interior think of it or, worse, Daoud Khan himself? Some settlement was clearly necessary, but reputations for honor also had to be upheld. Mediation was made more difficult for the mustufy by its public environment: Everywhere he and the

Takhar rais turned in search of privacy, a mass of other Takharis surrounded them. The conversation was itself like a buzkashi, with everyone pushing towards the center and shouting for attention. In this welter of noise, the following phrases are recognizable on tape:

Takhar Man: We too have a governor, a commandant, an announcer. Let one of *them* put us in jail.

Kunduz Mustufy: The rules are known.

Takhar: You put the rules under your feet.

Mustufy: O men of Takhar, I was your servant for four years. The respect I have for you made me rise from my seat and walk here. I cannot accept the thought that Takhar will be suspended for a year.

Takhar: Let him say two years.

Takhar: Three hundred thousand people in Takhar are interested in this game, and one man is ruining it. It's the wali the wali, the wali.

Mustufy: The wali had nothing to say about the decision. Here's a man not from Takhar and not from Kunduz [indicating the rais-i-buzkashi from nearby Baghlan who had come to assist in the reconciliation]. Let him speak. [He was given little or no chance.]

Takhar: If you give us our right, we are ready for playing. If not, we have not come for fighting.

Mustufy: Don't give yourselves a bad name. Do it for me.

Takhar: I am not a clown of the people.

Takhar: All right. Out of respect for the mustufy we give up our two points.

Takhar: For the sake of the Qur'an, give us one point.

Mustufy: If God is willing, you'll soon get ten points.

Takhar: We had not planned to return, but your intervention persuaded us. We do it in honor of you.

Mustufy: It is not good for a province to have a bad name.

Takhar: Who is this announcer who makes the scores?

(Note: Takhar here indicates not only the Takhar rais-i-buzkashi, but others from that province who were wrangling with the Kunduz mustufy.)

With the matter settled in terms of "respect," "honor," and "name," the Takhar rais and the Kunduz mustufy walked back across the field. Behind them came the entire Takhar contingent, and play was resumed with the original score unchanged at 5–2. No further disputes occurred, and Kunduz won on a spectacular last-minute score that provided, quite by chance, a most unusual moment of fieldwork experience.

The score came when Kunduz seemed finally to have lost the match, its unbeaten streak, and the championship. The leading Kunduz chapandaz singlehandedly took the calf around the flag and dropped it in the circle for a particularly stylish and all-important three-point play. Kunduz fans went wild. Several men ran onto the field, embraced the rider, and even draped their cloaks across his back. Nearly two dozen khans stepped forward to present him with money—and thus to have their names announced over the public address system.

Most remarkable of all, however, was the behavior of the wali. An instant after the score, I turned to look at him. For once, circumstances had overwhelmed the man. Far from seeming the deliberate, dispassionate, and nonpartisan tooi-wala, he was on his feet, waving his arms and shouting with everyone else. Our eyes met, but after the briefest moments intuition told me to look somewhere else. In the midst of a friendly reminiscence a month or so later, the wali smiled thinly and vouchsafed a rare revelation: "You know, I cursed you at that moment." I asked him why. "Because you looked at me when everyone else had his eyes on Ghafour [the chapandaz]." Again it seemed better not to pursue the issue. Other Afghan informants, however, immediately get the point: that I had been unwise enough to observe the wali in a state, as it were, of emotional nakedness. Only my foreignness, moreover, allowed him to take it lightly in retrospect. Rather like a game, I was—at least for my patron the wali— somewhere ambiguously between "for fun" and "for real."

A similar ambiguity hung over the tournament aftermath. On the one hand, it had been "only a game," and people had "had a good time." Less openly, there was much talk of the wali. Yes, he had managed some affairs very well, but, his critics were quick to suggest, he had tried to extend his authority too far. The Takhar game, they said, revealed its limits: He was, after all, the governor of only one province. A rumor spread that the Minister of the Interior had reprimanded him for provoking the Takhar walkout. Another, which gained credence among his supporters, was that the Minister had called instead to congratulate him.

I could not determine which, if either, story was true, but truth was itself little more than the totality of appearances. As winter finally gave way to spring and the buzkashi horses were pastured on the briefly green steppe, these impressions mingled with others in the structure of political reality. Ahead lay the oven-hot Central Asian summer with its scarce water and short tempers. This year the daytime fasts of Ramazan would add to the tinderbox quality of day-to-day life. In the dynamics of inevitable conflict, memories of the past buzkashi season would impress themselves, at whatever level of consciousness, on the minds of all concerned. Among khans, a successful wintertime tooi-wala can more readily mobilize summer support in irrigation disputes. Increasingly, however, the significant struggle is between whole modes of political organization: the government and the khans.

As a publicly observable index to the state of this competition, the events of a Kunduz buzkashi season had revealed the greater authority of government. This revelation, in turn, had enhanced that authority all the more. Despite the foibles of an exuberantly forceful wali—or, rather, in part on account of his very arbitrariness—the impression of government control had grown throughout the province. Now private individuals, the khans especially, would be that much less evasive when confronted by cadastral surveys, conscription deadlines, tax notices, and criminal enquiries. Compliance would remain far from complete, but buzkashi recollections would play a subtle role in its increase.

KABUL BUZKASHI

The annual tournament in Kabul completes the process of buzkashi routinization. If things can occasionally go wrong on afternoons in provincial centers, the twelve-day national championship is celebrated exactly as planned. Year after year, the tournament has taken place with a sense of scheduled regularity not at all characteristic of unruly Afghanistan. Elaborate in scope, it amounts to a national tooi analogous in many respects to the much smaller-scale, khan-sponsored extravaganzas. Now the buzkashi experience is not only more extended, but also more standardized in terms of time, space, and participants. As always, the status of sponsor is central, and in Kabul it is personified by the Head of State. As always, the buzkashi sponsorship is only as effective as the support it can command.

In Kabul this support is at its most secure. Whereas a traditional tooi-wala has only an ad hoc "action-set" and a provincial wali his patchwork of transient subordinates, the Kabul buzkashi qaum represents a well developed bureaucracy of permanent specialists. Here the ANOC is in its capital city element, and its career officials are guaranteed the cooperation of other government organs. Prominent among these are the Ministries of Defense and the Interior with their particularly elitist professional staffs. For more than a quarter century, patterns of bureaucratic interaction have been refined. These arrangements tend to survive changes in regime, when top officials are purged but subordinates remain.

On the basis of such continuity, most important issues are decided by simple precedent: when to start the tournament, how many days to let it run, whom to invite/summon, and so forth. This last matter has evolved over the years to reflect political development in the North. In 1953, only two teams took part: Qataghan and Turkestan. Each represented a vast and, at that time, unsectioned area. After the partition of 1964, eight provincial teams took part. By

THE KABUL TOURNAMENT. On Opening Day in 1976, two provincial teams compete in Ghazi Stadium. Police line the concrete retaining wall. The VIP pavilion stands on the far side.

1975, the number had reached ten, with the introduction of buzkashi to a pair of Hindu Kush provinces.[6]

In midsummer, when extreme heat makes buzkashi seem impossibly remote, the first official notifications are sent from the ANOC to the Ministry of the Interior and thence to the ten provincial walis. In most instances, the governor then delegates his rais-i-buzkashi to organize what in theory amounts to an all-star team. Problems often arise at this point. While authority is well specified in the Kabul bureaucracy, its locus remains problematic when the khans try to settle on a team. Much depends on whether they have really chosen their rais-i-buzkashi themselves or have had him foisted on them by an importunate wali. Sometimes, as in Kunduz in the fall of 1976, the wali may simply select the provincial team himself. The means of selection can be consequential later in Kabul, when arbitrarily structured teams are said to lack *e'tifaq* or cooperation.

However constituted, a team is always produced by each province. Not to do so in normal times would be unthinkable. The tournament is, after all, lots of fun. Buzkashi horsemen anticipate Kabul every year as a kind of recreational field trip near harvest time: a big-city fling after months of rural responsibility. Despite some misgivings about abuse of their horses and the vague recognition that they themselves are left more than ever on the sidelines, most horse-own-ing khans actively want to go. The presentation of a team on sched-ule is guaranteed, furthermore, by a grudging respect for government authority: unwise is the province that fails to supply a team for the national tooi.

Before the Salang Pass tunnel was dug through the Hindu Kush in 1963, the buzkashi contingents would travel from the North on horseback. Originally they would ride into Kabul with great pag-eantry over flower-strewn streets.[7] Now, arrivals are more mundane. Most teams can be transported by lorry in a day from their home provinces. Once in Kabul, each provincial group is allocated the same sector of a vast campground every year. Large signs, printed in the politically dominant but essentially non-northern language of Pushtu, designate provincial space. Nearby are Ghazi Stadium, where the games are played, and a mess hall where meals are served to certified provincial group members. The entire tournament com-plex exists under government auspices and is guarded by uniformed troops. The Northerners may come and go from their campground at will, but government presence is ubiquitous.

Several days before the tournament starts, the ten provincial buzkashi rais troop to the ANOC offices. The meeting that follows could hardly be less like its analogue at a traditional tooi. The robed and turbaned (and, in many cases, illiterate) khans are met by busi-ness-suited bureaucrats with lists whose details have already been determined. Schedules are announced, and procedures are reviewed. The hubbub of a tooi-khana discussion is entirely absent. Indeed, there is little discussion at all: The officials talk and the khans listen.

The last day prior to the tournament is devoted almost entirely to rehearsal of the official presentation ceremony. Morning and after-noon, all the members of all ten teams parade on horseback in and out of Ghazi Stadium. Now high-ranking army officers help the ANOC staff with supervision, and the exercise seems almost like a military drill. Every step, salute, and bow is repeated to perfection. Chapandazan privately complain that this extended rehearsal tires them and their mounts, but sponsorship priorities are already evi-dent: predictably flawless ceremony even at the expense of competi-tive performance.

Established months in advance, the first day of the tournament arrives with considerable media fanfare. Radio Afghanistan and the various government newspapers frequently include the phrase "according to schedule" to emphasize the theme of predictability. Otherwise, first-day media attention concentrates on the Head of State tooi-wala who is almost always in attendance. From regime to regime, the national tournament serves to recognize this central figure as the paramount khan in Afghanistan. Glossy program covers from the monarchy era read, "On the occasion of the birthday of His Majesty the King," with a color portrait of Zahir Shah in military regalia on the inside. The 1967 version includes a full page of large gilt lettering. Again the message is written in Pushtu:

> It is the King who safeguards the national sovereignty, and he is the supporter of democratic evolution. He is responsible for the pres- ervation of independence and national integrity. We firmly believe that the King is the torchbearer of any progressive movement.

As the minutes tick away in the early afternoon of Day One, the 18,000 stadium seats gradually fill until, at the designated time, one empty place remains for the Head of State.

Ghazi Stadium, named in honor of independence-era martyrs, is itself a testimony to power of central government. It stands on an utterly flat plain near the Kabul River, and as such its very existence owes nothing to natural topography. Rather, it represents the willful capacity of government to impose itself on the environment. Second in cultural bulk only to the ancient Bala Hissar fortress, the stadium dominates a nearly vacant corner of Kabul. Its architecture presents a great advance on the geometric precision suggested at the Kunduz buzkashi grounds. Here concrete combines with metal and glass to create an entire setting of flat planes, smooth arcs, and regular angles. Most significantly of all, the play area is now enclosed on all

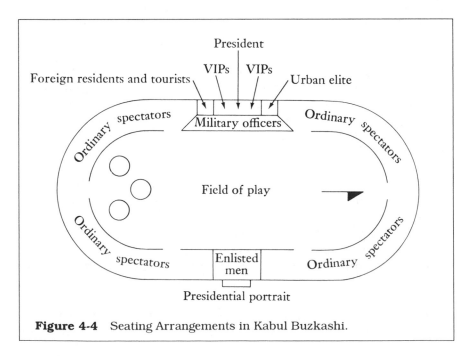

Figure 4-4   Seating Arrangements in Kabul Buzkashi.

sides by a waist-high, concrete retaining wali. Six portals provide the only points of legitimate access to the even, grassy surface.

Seating arrangements in Kabul are likewise precisely delineated (see figure 4-4). The one empty seat at 2:29 P.M. on Day One of the 1977 tournament was located in the center of an elevated pavilion canopied in purple. Otherwise, the pavilion was full of national-level VIPs: presidential family members, cabinet ministers, military generals, and foreign ambassadors. Directly across the field loomed an immense color portrait of Daoud, whose expression implied a kind of casual forcefulness. To the left of the VIP pavilion sat members of the Afghan urban elite whose 50-afghani tickets distanced them from the rank and file. On the other side of the VIPs a couple of hundred foreign residents occupied complimentary seats, which henceforth would be ticketed to tourists at 500 afghanis apiece. The ANOC officials (scorers, timekeepers, and announcers) sat at their table in one corner of this section. Members of the Afghan armed forces attended free as guests, in effect, of the tooi-wala/Head of State whose authority ultimately depended on their support. Appropriately, their seats were located directly beneath his. Officers sat underneath the VIP pavilion, and enlisted men crowded below the presidential portrait. Both, of course, were in uniform. Ordinary spectators occupied the other three-quarters of Ghazi Stadium. Here sat men (and a very few women) from all segments of Afghan life. Most were Kabulis, but many came from Pushtun areas further south. Sprinkled among them were nonplaying members of the ten provincial buzkashi groups: the khans and their grooms. For them the normal ten-afghani entry fee had been waived, but otherwise these traditional figures went unrecognized.

At 2:30 sharp the President arrived. All those in the VIP pavilion rose, and the announcer proclaimed the event in patriotic terms over the public address system. The national anthem was broadcast over powerful loudspeakers. Two identical columns of horsemen rode onto the field for the much rehearsed presentation ceremony: the umpires (who had abandoned their everyday status as military officers to assume a critical tooi-bashi role), the provincial rais in order of the previous year's finish, trumpeters and drummers who provided a somewhat somber march, and finally the teams of chapandazan each led by its deputy rais. The formation paraded around the oval and faced the President. The music ceased, and all the horsemen simultaneously saluted Daoud: the umpires in standard military fashion, the rais with a dip of their distinctive provincial banners, and everyone else with a rise in the stirrups and a bow. The head umpire rode forward and received Presidential permission to start, whereupon the formation marched off the field. Moments later, the two teams first scheduled to play duly made their appearance. A whistle blew, and the initial game got underway.

Two categories of personnel had been eliminated in the refinement of this ceremony from Kunduz to Kabul. In the national tournament there are no longer any extraneous sawarkaran horsemen. Each team consists of a rais, his deputy, and ten chapandazan. Otherwise, only the umpires are allowed on the field of play. The town crier is likewise missing. Integral to a tooi and welcome in the provincial context as a source of comic relief, this traditional figure has now been replaced completely by the public address system with its professional announcers and powerful equipment. Their message, however bland by comparison with town crier praise chants, echoes all across the stadium in the two national languages of Pushtu and Dari (with occasional explanatory tidbits in stilted English for the foreigners). None of the Turkic dialects native to most northern horsemen is ever employed.

Now on ANOC home ground, the tournament matches adhere strictly to qarajai rules, and buzkashi completes its transformation from game to sport. Bounded on all sides in space by the concrete wall, it is timed with a stopwatch. Team uniforms for the chapandazan are, finally, uniform. The rais and their deputies wear corduroy outfits of brilliant red, a color ordinarily considered far too flashy for deliberate khans, but obviously of spectacle value here. The umpires wear less outlandish dress: dark brown tunics and trousers with a green sash symbolic of accord. Play moves back and forth between the circles and the far flag, with what many spectators find to be an increasingly repetitive quality. Some matches are close and thus contain a measure of suspense. Spectacular shows of horsemanship can occur at any time. For the most part, however, only the northern aficionados follow play with real intentness after the first few minutes.

Scores are recorded in summary fashion. The head umpire, the successful chapandaz, and his rais ride to a point directly below the ANOC table. The umpire calls the names of the chapandaz and, sometimes, his horse-owner khan to the announcer, who repeats them over the microphone with the current score. Here more often than in Kunduz, the name of the khan is omitted. Nor does he appear for even the brief moment of bonus presentation. The traditional patrons of buzkashi remain buried in the crowd while all glory in the first-order game goes to their chapandazan.

No other order of game is allowed to take place in any problematic sense. Disputes, when they occur at all, are muted at the time and settled later in the privacy of an ANOC office. Very occasionally, an ANOC official may have to walk onto the field as a reminder to the

PRAYER AT HALFTIME. Beneath a portrait of President Daoud, the pious face toward Mecca in 1977. A year later, Daoud was dead and his portrait ▶ replaced by that of Taraki.

chapandazan of their situation. The concrete wall inhibits unauthorized intrusions. At the Kabul tournament, as one informant mused afterwards in his northern home, "Only a madman would feel free to do whatever came into his head." In 1977, precisely this sort of lunatic trespass occurred. The Baghlan provincial contingent had been accompanied by a recognized eccentric who used to walk into the thick of tooi play and trust, as he put it, "to the grace of God." At a government game in Kunduz, he wandered onto the field several times, was ordered back by the announcer, but clownishly ignored the commands and was finally allowed to stay. Not so in Kabul. No sooner had he climbed the barricade and started to stroll towards the action than uniformed policemen returned him bodily to the stands. There he was permitted to stay for the afternoon, but clearly there would be no exceptions to the system. Only his buffoonlike manner had saved him from serious consequences. The only other occasion when spatial boundaries are blurred occurs at halftime of the second contest each afternoon, when several hundred especially pious spectators pour over the wall, spread cloths on the field, and pray in unison towards Mecca. Tolerated in 1976, this practice was at first opposed by authorities in 1977. Individual policemen were unsure, however, of which master to serve—Allah or the ANOC—and the new policy was allowed to lapse.

Games end as routinely as they begin. The whistle blows, the two teams again assemble to face the VIP pavilion, and the whole formation parades demurely off the field. Day after day, two matches are

PRESIDENTIAL CONGRATULATIONS. Daoud prepares to embrace a chapandaz of the winning 1976 Balkh team. Defense Minister Rassouli and ANOC officials look on.

played and their results totaled. All awards are deferred until after the tournament finishes. In both 1976 and 1977, President Daoud was absent every day after the first but returned on the final afternoon for the championship playoff matches. At their close, all ten teams made a last ceremonial appearance, and the provincial winners (Balkh in 1976, Jowzjan in 1977) walked upstairs with the ten rais to shake hands with Daoud and have imitation gold medals hung around their necks.

A more comprehensive awards ceremony takes place after dinner on this last day, when the three hundred-odd certified horsemen from the North meet with tournament officials in a nearby auditorium. In 1977 the ten provincial contingents (each with a rais, a deputy, ten khans, ten chapandazan, and ten grooms) barged into the auditorium lobby to escape the evening chill and milled buzkashi-like against each other. Suddenly a lone army officer blew his whistle for silence and peremptorily ordered the horsemen to sit on the bare stone floor. Compliance was immediate and universal. Some of the greatest khans in northern Afghanistan could only sit and listen as the officer directed each contingent to its designated rows.

The first two rows of auditorium seats were reserved for government officials. Bare-headed and Western-dressed, they orchestrated the ceremony: national anthem, nationalistic speeches, and finally a sequence of standardized rewards whose value bore no reference to the order of tournament finish. All rais received blankets; all khans medals; all chapandazan and grooms sums of money. The main speech came from the Minister of Defense, who also served as honorary national buzkashi chairman. The Republic, he intoned, was responsible for all good things in general and for the growth of buzkashi in particular. The development of the game was like the development of all Afghanistan in an era of progress under Daoud Khan. Cooperation was essential to both domains. Some teams—he knew which ones they were—had not cooperated with their rais, and their resultant poor play had been all too evident. Led by the front rows of Kabul officials, the Northerners had little option but to applaud whenever the name of Daoud was mentioned. Finally, the Minister advised, "You should return to your provinces with the Republic in mind. On my behalf, be sure to greet your governors and subgovernors." With the substance of the ceremony at an end—and since, after all, the occasion was supposed to be fun—the horsemen were at long last treated to a live concert of Radio Afghanistan musicians.

By noon the next day, buzkashi has left Kabul. By dark, many of the horsemen are already at home with tales of their urban adventure. In remote guest houses lit by candles or imported gas lamps, the travelers recount their activities of each day to spellbound audiences: the trip to the Kabul River Gorge where the government has a great dam, the amble through an old bazaar only to find a new set of traffic lights, even the visit to the zoo where Khair Mohammed played chapandaz on the back of an elephant until the keeper came and almost had him arrested. Many of the stories deal in traditional fashion with the buzkashi. It is still very much of interest whose horse played at all and, even more, played well. Certain memorable chapandaz exploits are recounted in ever more vivid detail. There are, however, no buzkashi disputes to discuss and dissect. Whether about the tournament itself or some random event in Kabul, the recollections are set against a background of government authority.

Some khans feel vaguely cheated. The Kabul tournament, many say, is no good for their horses: The weather is still too hot; the limit on substitution compounds this temperature problem; and the concrete wall can maim or kill. The ANOC stipend never covers expenses. And all for what? To be told what to do by people who have never been to a real buzkashi. Even so, it was fun to go to Kabul and good to be on cooperative terms with the provincial wali. Fulfilled or not, most khans will want to do it again next year.

Back in Kabul, other government branches further the process of impression management. Press and radio represent the tournament as an event spectacular, but predictable. Invariably, the bottom line praises the Head of State whose celebratory initiative has been so successful. From regime to regime, the government agency Afghan Films produces documentaries of the Kabul buzkashi. With my fieldwork still in its initial phase, I was given a chance to view the rushes of a new Daoudian version in the fall of 1976. A member of the production staff was graciously provided to answer my questions. No sound track other than martial music had been dubbed as yet, and the two of us talked intermittently. The film content itself was about equally divided between buzkashi action and the presence of Daoud. A chapandaz would score, and the President would applaud in lordly confirmation. At one point I casually asked my companion his qaum and his residence. The response was immediate: "My qaum is Afghan, and my residence is Afghanistan."

"Yes," said I, "but . . . "

"No but," he said. "You've read too many old books. The longer you stay here, the more you'll realize that since the Republican revolution we are all one qaum and one nation. To think otherwise is out of date."[8]

NOTES

[1]Cohen, Abner, *Two-Dimensional Man* (London: Routledge and Kegan Paul, 1974), p. 31.

[2]More precisely, the seven minor pavilions or camps are associated with the five subprovincial districts (Chardara, Dasht-i-Archi, Imam Sahib,

Khanabad, and Qala-i-Zol), one more minor district (Aliabad), and the Spinzar Company, a government-run manufacturing firm with quasi-political staus.

[3]On the occasion of the Muslim New Year—March 21, 1977—President of the Republic Mohammed Daoud Khan made one of his infrequent journeys outside the capital city of Kabul. His destination in this instance was the city of Mazar-i-Sharif, capital of Balkh Province, and traditional center of New Year festivities. The President delivered a patriotic message at the morning ceremony, flew by helicopter to the neighboring province of Jowzjan, with its important natural gasworks, and returned to Mazar-i-Sharif, where the afternoon buzkashi was kept waiting an hour and a half for his arrival. Characteristically, all attention was centered on him, and precautions were taken to ensure that events transpired according to plan.

Several visitors from other provinces remarked, however, that the sense of control achieved was less than anticipated. The nonplaying sawarkaran were not all kept in their place beyond the boundaries of play. The tanker truck full of water that was meant to dampen the dust failed to sprinkle properly. Finally and most remarkably, play was completely interrupted at one point as 50 or 60 adolescent boys poured onto the field riding donkeys and contending in buzkashi style for a sheepskin. The Balkh provincial authorities were at first outraged at this indiscretion, whose scope was made all the more apparently disastrous by the presidential presence. The Balkh rais-i-buzkashi and his deputies tried, without immediate effect, to disperse the youthful interlopers. Their embarrassment was thus compounded by frustration, until it was realized that the President was immensely amused by this bit of spontaneity. Immediately, anger changed to encouragement as the official competition was suspended and the boys permitted to play on donkeyback. Even here, however, the provincial officials attempted to control the situation by getting a more or less standardized game going.

Outsiders remarked, both at the time and afterwards, that although the donkeyback buzkashi was fun, the entire enterprise had not been sufficiently well controlled and that it therefore reflected adversely on Balkh Province, its officials, and its citizens. Balkh, it was said, had not succeeded in controlling its own undertaking.

[4]The newness of certain conceptual elements in qarajai buzkashi is evidenced in the adoption of English words to express them. These occur in the dimensions of time, space, and personnel. In the tudabarai form as played at a tooi, there is no significant sense of "halftime," "out" (of bounds), or "team." All three words have been adopted into the qarajai form along with "Coca-Cola" and "Fanta," which the chapandazan drink at halftime.

[5]Clearly the shotgun represented more than a merely ceremonial mace, and quite likely the wali had some similar weapon in hand when he died in the Ningarhar Government House shootout fourteen months later (see chapter 5). What would have been the reaction if he had used it at the tooi? Would the people have said, "Right, such is the way of walis," and acquiesced, or would they have attacked him in righteous anger? My guess in this instance is that it would have depended on the number of soldiers he had with him. Coercion, in other words, and not legitimacy was the immediate

mainstay of his authority. On the other hand, the Daoud regime (unlike its successors) was regarded as more or less legitimate on the level of national affairs. Even in the hinterland, such a level is known to exist, and the right for a central government to function in it is generally acknowledged. The issue of legitimacy in the era of Daoud was not whether he was the rightful head of state or whether his walis were rightfully appointed, but whether—or rather to what extent—the regime could rightfully intrude beneath the national level into the day-to-day lives of individuals.

[6]The eight teams that have played since 1964 are all representative of provinces from north of the Hindu Kush: Badakhshan, Baghlan, Balkh, Faryab, Jowzjan, Kunduz, Samangan, and Takhar. Bamian and Parwan, both mountain provinces with no native buzkashi tradition, began sending (unsuccessful) teams in 1975.

[7]For an excellent fictional account of the first Kabul buzkashi see Kessel, Joseph, *The Horsemen* (New York: Farrar, Straus and Giroux, 1968).

[8]Qaum may have been out of date in 1976 Kabul, but exiles from the Turkic North felt otherwise. Soon after publication (1982) the first edition of this book was read and approved, but also critiqued by a Turkman who had emigrated from Andkhoi, in northernmost Afghanistan, in the 1950s. A former schoolteacher among his own people, he had run afoul of the central government because of his ethnic sentiments. Like many other Turkic speakers, he still dreamed of an independent Turkestan. His marginal notes urge me to use Turkic (rather than Persian) terms and to report the Kabul government suppressions of Turkoman and Uzbek buskashis in the countryside.

5

A GOAT BETWEEN TWO LIONS

> How can a small power like Afghanistan, which is like a goat between two lions, or a grain of wheat between two strong mill-stones of the grinding mill, stand in the midway of the stones without being ground to dust?
>
> —Amir Abdur Rahman Khan, 1900

"What is it that's going on here?" If the question still nags, it is because of a pervasive discrepancy. On the one hand, many informants—especially those with political prominence—maintain abstractly that buzkashi entails no more than simple recreation. Only a game, they say, which merely gets the people together and gives them some fun. Rural khans, Kunduz officials, and ANOC functionaries all patted my queries on the head and advised that I stick to issues of equine diet and chapandaz technique.

Obviously their position reflects one side of the truth. "Gets the people together and gives them some fun" suggests that benignly integrative function that sponsors proclaim in tooi invitations, provincial public address announcements, and national press releases. Whichever the level of buzkashi, its social context bespeaks celebration as participants gather and mingle on avowed terms of good-natured friendship. The tooi occasion, again at whichever level, gains further integrative effect from the association of buzkashi with cultural heritage. To fun and friendship is added the vital ingredient of forefathers. A national tournament brochure (printed for the literate tourist audience) introduces "Afghanistan's National Sport":

> Exclusively Afghan, Buzkashi as it is played today reflects the boldness and fierce competitive spirit of the Afghan people. The origins of the game, however, are obscure.

109

> The great equestrian tradition out of which buzkashi developed and without which it would fade goes back as far as the time of Alexander the Great.
>
> Expert horsemen, nomads of northern Afghanistan, fought Alexander's hitherto triumphant army to a standstill. When the ancient Greeks first saw these formidable and accomplished horsemen of Central Asia, they believed the legend of the centaur (half horse half man) had materialized. For any witness of modern Buzkashi, such a reaction is easily understood. Before moving on to India, Alexander replenished his cavalry with this sturdy breed of horse.
>
> Many people associate Buzkashi with the notorious Genghis Khan. Actually, the Mongol horsemen were adept at advancing on enemy campsites and, without dismounting, swooping up sheep, goats, and other pillage at full gallop. In retaliation, the inhabitants of northern Afghanistan established a mounted defense against the raids and this practice might be the direct fore-bearer [*sic*] of today's Buzkashi.

Although written for foreign consumption, the passage generally coincides with domestic beliefs about buzkashi. Values and history (however dubious in details) combine to integrate participants in what the government phrases here as part of the national patrimony.

Most of those who describe buzkashi in such mildly constructive and conflict-free terms are essentially honest and open in this attitude. No doubt some men—especially officials of the recent communist regimes in their quest for legitimacy—consciously manipulate the game for political purposes, but these constitute a minority overall. Even most sponsors are probably unaware of their own ulterior motives much of the time. For them as for their guests, the entire buzkashi experience primarily represents a special brand of social gathering, both venerable and spectacular, in which all participants are temporarily bound together by their shared separation from mundane life.

All well and good (and undeniably true), but such an exclusively integrative analysis fails to answer a further question: Under whose authority does the integration occur? This question could usefully be asked of all institutions everywhere which seek to enhance sentiments of commonality. Even the most egalitarian of undertakings requires some degree of leadership. In some societies, admittedly, such leadership conveys relatively little authority beyond the activity for which it is specified. Successful leadership of a local Independence Day celebration in the United States does not necessarily signal a gain in command over wider affairs. In Afghanistan, however, where the locus of authority is so chronically insecure, any social initiative has political connotations, and all men observe its process carefully. Whoever can exercise authority over an undertaking—no matter how superficially apolitical its nature—enhances his reputation for command.

Despite protestations, so it is with buzkashi. These very protestations spring from the ambiguity of games and are necessary if that ambiguity is to be preserved. Indeed, the protestations are necessary to the game itself. Were there only the one political perspective, the dispute-ridden buzkashi of rural tooi would be truly warlike, and thus impossible to play. Similarly the strictly controlled buzkashis of Kabul would be understood as mere parades and so forfeit all claim to authentic attention. Instead, the effect of national tournaments rests on an awareness whose development must be extremely subtle. As Cohen observes,

> Symbols are essential for the maintenance and development of the social order. To do their job efficiently, their social functions must remain largely unconscious and unintended by the actors. Once their functions become known to the actors, the symbols lose a great deal of their efficacy.[1]

James Peacock makes much the same case for artistic activity, which, as a category distinguished by indirect "modes of influence," extends quite readily to games and buzkashi:

One might even argue that art works a powerful influence on society precisely because its modes of influence are undercover. By being unsuspected, artistic influences might be more powerful than the religious ones everyone is aware of (and therefore on guard against). Religion makes no bones about the social message it preaches, but by publicly claiming that art carries no social message (art for art's sake) the artist may increase acceptance of the social message (influence) that art, in fact, does carry. This is not to say that the artist deliberately works it so that his art will have powerful social impact. As is well known, symbols have latent function.[2]

All the points that Peacock makes for art apply to buzkashi as well. His concept, furthermore, of "symbolic action" has dual relevance. Buzkashi, first, is a prism-like condensation (rather than simply a mirrored reflection) of two complementary social themes: respect for the past with its emphasis on assertively masculine values, and awareness of the dark uncontrollability that lurks below surface calm. Second, buzkashi qualifies as an "active agency within society" that molds, however subtly, the political opinions of its participants.

Peacock's work deals not with games but with art in the form of theatrical material. And yet that rehearsed, set-piece process of theater is consistent with the predictability of Kabul buzkashi. In its extreme routinization, the national tournament approaches completely scripted performance. All sense of the problematic is confined to the first-order game, and the resultant impression corresponds to government design.

The same is true to lesser extents in the other two buzkashi contexts as sponsors (the tooi-wala and the provincial wali) attempt to stage their own shows. In their cases, qaum resources of authority are scarcer and less secure. Things go wrong, and the best-laid integrative plans abruptly disintegrate. Subsequent disputes conform to the "social dramas" of Victor Turner: "public episodes of tensional eruptions" which, whether reconciled or not, alter the field in which they occur.[3]

Turner's recognition of "public episodes" as causative factors revives another bothersome issue. If the nature of buzkashi experience must finally be described in terms of frame ambiguity, what can be said of buzkashi consequences? Do specific buzkashi activities, even in the angry extreme of social drama, really alter the contextual field? In the terms of this study, what effect do events of the first three orders of game have on their fourth-order counterpart of real-world politics?

The reiteration of an early disclaimer is appropriate here: It is virtually impossible to "prove" any isolated causal link. The very ambiguity of buzkashi significance—the latency of its symbolic functions—precludes specific documentation of cause and effect. At best, the relationship must be inferred. With that limitation in mind, the argument now returns to its database of individual actors at a moment about to turn tumultuous and catastrophic.

Conducted from late 1976 to early 1978, this study was informed by the lives of a number of specific people. Some were men of little worldly status: a privately kept mullah, one gentle and long-suffering groom, the town crier whose antics enlivened most area toois, several chapandazan whose fame was buzkashi based. Whatever their virtues, these were essentially men of small repute. As such, when this chapter was first written (1981), I had scant information about them. Some reappear in chapter 6 and the epilogue.

Of more political substance are the subsequent careers of "men with names": several old-line khans, one provincial rais-i-buzkashi, the wali of Kunduz, the ANOC president in Kabul, and finally, if for me at a distance, the Minister of Defense and the President of the Republic. All of these men were once identified with buzkashi success. Most were successful sponsors. What has happened to them in the interim?

The greater the names, of course, the more is known about what happened during and after the disastrous April 1978 Saur Revolution. At first there was little news about the rural khans. Though well known in local society, their names never reached the foreign press, and exile rumors often amounted to fanciful speculation. Gradually a pattern emerged whereby, in a world turned upside down, it was better *not* to have a name, given most of the rural khans were targets, albeit to varying degrees, of the new Marxist policies.

Some of the smaller fry hunkered down and were overlooked. A few khans collaborated with the regime. Many more opposed it actively or passively. Some were killed. Some came with families and followers to Pakistan as refugees. Some of these then went back to join the jihad in Afghanistan but not as important leaders. As a class the rural khans of my 1970s acquaintance were now largely superseded by a younger generation of self-made military commanders who, with new skills and energies, were better able to provide newly crucial spoils (weapons and money) from outside. Their involvement as new buzkashi sponsors is discussed in chapter 6.

Here I deal first with the rise and fall of a rather more anomalous character: myself. Unlike those of the other men, my story lacks both heights of prestige and depths of tragedy, but it does indicate a pattern: that the more widely a name is known, the more its owner must be prepared for risk as well as reward; and that reputation acquired at a buzkashi game, while immediately helpful, is by itself no ultimate guarantee of security.

What could be called my public—even, in a very broad sense, political—career as a fieldworker started on Friday, February 18, 1977, at the Kunduz government game dedicated to the formal election of President Daoud. Still new and unknown in the province, I had taken residence with its rais-i-buzkashi, who on that auspicious day had volunteered to supply all the necessary resources: calf carcass, prizes, and refreshments. Intent on enhancing my relationship with the rais, I suggested to his nephew the possibility of my making a 1,000 afghani ($21) contribution to the effort. The nephew, himself a khan of considerable standing, insisted instead that I present the money to the wali to be offered as a special prize. "That way," he said, "everyone will be happy and not only the rais. The wali will be happy. Everyone will be happy. Furthermore, everyone will know who you are. They will all know your name."

At the time, it seemed an inspired suggestion. I took a new 1,000-afghani note (the largest currency denomination), put it in an envelope, and wrote a flowery Persian inscription on the outside. Shortly after the buzkashi began, I gave the envelope to the wali without a word. Immediately he motioned for the announcer, and a moment later the public address system blared:

> Honored friends, a foreigner, an American, Mr. Whitney Azoy, has offered 1,000 afghanis as a prize in the name of Mohammed Daoud Khan. He has offered a prize of 1,000 afghanis. He has written, "On the occasion of the election of the first President of the Republic of Afghanistan." All of us owe applause for Mr. Azoy. [Applause] Mr. Azoy is here to learn about buzkashi. His presentation proves that the name of Mohammed Daoud is known not only in Afghanistan but throughout the world by everyone. [Applause] All of us owe applause for Mr. Azoy. [Applause].

The short-range consequences of my initiative were very gratifying to the ego of a novice anthropologist far from home. Overnight I found myself much more generally known in Kunduz town and, as such, distinguished from other foreigners who came as tourists for a day or two. Favors were done, offers were made, and credit was extended. More to the point, my relationship with the wali became quite close. I was welcome, he said, to be with him anytime, whether at his home or at his office. I was his "guest" and so had the run of the province. On several other ritual occasions he arranged for me to be situated in a prominent place. I, for my part, did what I could to maintain this closeness: being both deferential and familiar in a fashion possible only for foreigners whose social significance is never quite real, bringing him token but hard-to-get gifts from the American Commissary in Kabul, and making a modest contribution to the building of a Khanabad mosque which had become known as one of his personal initiatives.

Unfortunately for me, there was also a second, longer-range consequence. In November 1977, I was bluntly refused an extension to my research visa. To make matters more frustrating, no explanation was offered by the Ministry of Foreign Affairs in Kabul. Kunduz friends, however, agree with regard to a most likely scenario. I had indeed, they say, become well known. Much of my reputation in the province was associated with the wali. In the summer of 1977, however, he was transferred to another province. Following his departure ceremonies in which I was conspicuously included, his successor refused to recognize my existence at all. Twice I attempted a courtesy call only to be rebuffed by the same office staff which had previously proven so friendly. Not realizing the implications, I simply remained in Kunduz and went about my work. Almost certainly, however, the change in governors led to my not being granted the visa extension. The gubernatorial shift signaled to everybody (except my ignorant self) a shift in political alignments. Each wali in turn tries to make a name for himself and does so in part through opposing the clients, enterprises, and policies of his predecessor. Other political actors in Kunduz thus quite likely perceived in my presence an opportunity to curry favor with the new man, and so represented me to him as a suspiciously credentialed protégé of his predecessor. This information (with whatever further embellishments) was probably passed to Kabul when I applied for the renewal.

The departure of the wali also resulted in the status loss of another of his clients (and my immediate patron/host), the rais-i-buzkashi himself. First selected by the former wali over the heads of his fellow khans, the rais now had a problem similar to mine. Emboldened by the studied indifference of the new wali to buzkashi, an interest identified with his predecessor and so avoided by him, rival khans made trouble for the rais from the autumn Kabul tournament onwards. The team "lacked cooperation," played fitfully, and, after its much celebrated runner-up finish the year before, dropped to a lowly sixth place overall. A month later at the first tooi of the winter, a dispute led to outright fighting, and the rais was hospitalized for two weeks. (I was busy at the time fighting my own visa battles and so must rely here on the firsthand accounts of friends, that is, on precisely the sort of impressionistic reports which form the day-to-day currency of politics). When, the consensus story proceeds, he later sought redress from the new governor, he was told to get out, go home, and give the position to someone who could handle it. The deposed rais "has fallen lower than where he was in the first place. Only his really close friends still call him 'rais sahib.'"

For the rais and me, life went on: He was embarrassed (in a society where embarrassment can be tantamount to political impotence); I, a transient, was merely inconvenienced. For the men in this study with really great names, the future seemed quite serene. Certainly the Kabul tournament of October 1977 had gone without the suggestion of a hitch. Its thousands of participants could hardly have been unimpressed by the pervasive display of government authority. Consciously or otherwise, all had taken these impressions home with them.

Perhaps least convinced, however, by such displays were the relatively sophisticated Kabul politicians—civilian and military, in office and out—who have closest access to national power. These men remain immune to the illusions of fixed authority that every regime tries to generate. Undeterred by the stuff of buzkashi impressions, they realize that power at the national level is not so quantifiably a matter of numbered supporters from urban bazaars and rural hamlets. A set-piece production like the Kabul buzkashi would become politically significant to them only if something went very wrong and the government lost control. Otherwise, these modern opportunists concede the regime its display and concentrate instead on qualitative resources. In advance calculations of coup possibilities, the critical factor is not how many men, but who and where placed and with what special skills.

The coup of April 27, 1978, is history. Daoud had failed to provide sufficient spoils for a critical element in his political qaum: the leftists who had facilitated his own takeover five years earlier. Suddenly, to recall the grim reaction of my Afghan friend at the airport, the real buzkashi had begun. The three men with the greatest names in my fieldwork died violently at the outset: President of the Republic Mohammed Daoud, Minister of Defense Gholam Haidar Rassouli, and former Governor of Kunduz (then Governor of more strategic and prestigious Ningarhar) Abdul Khaleq Rafiqi. In December the wali had shown me the machine gunner sentries outside his newly occupied Government House, but I do not know which way their barrels were turned in April. The ANOC president was more fortunate. Despite his membership in the Mohammedzai clan that had dominated national politics for more than a century, he was merely removed from his position and at last report was, euphemistically, "at home."

Six months later after a summer of incipient civil war, the new regime of Mohammed Noor Taraki took special pains to fulfill the annual expectation for a Kabul buzkashi. Its resources already stretched by various hinterland rebellions, the government spared no expense in an all-out attempt at impression management. Several ill-advised efforts to revise basic elements of symbolic culture—national flag, national anthem, mode of address, and, most of all, Islam—had given particular offense, and the national tournament offered a means of regaining lost ground. Furthermore, a strictly controlled tooi of at least the usual scope would serve, as always, to display political authority.

Indeed, the express intention was for a better-than-ever tooi. On the day before it began, the government *Kabul Times* enthused with a political zeal that outran English grammar:

> The Olympic Association of Afghanistan is taking necessary mea-sures for holding the grand championship which will be held in a more grandeur [sic] manner than the previous years."[4]

The format, in fact, was virtually the same as in the past. The Head of State presided with much fanfare on the first day. A picture of Taraki had replaced that of Daoud opposite the VIP pavilion, and two other likenesses of the new national khan adorned the end sections. In a move perhaps calculated to placate Muslim sentiment, no attempt was made to keep worshippers from the field at halftime.

At the end of the tournament, its regime sponsorship took special advantage of this traditional institution to make a series of modern points. A new Minister of the Interior presided at the auditorium awards session and delivered the main speech on behalf of "the eternal Saur [the month in which the coup occurred] Revolution which will work for the development of sport especially the ancient buzkashi as it envisages bringing fundamental changes in other social, economic, and cultural fields."[5]

This year, moreover, the final matches were preceded by a Presidential audience for the northern horsemen at the House of the People (formerly the Republican Palace, formerly the Royal Palace). The *Kabul Times* lead story carried the entire Taraki speech with pictures of himself and applauding chapandazan (in buzkashi dress) beneath the headline, "Great Leader speaks to heroic horsemen." His speech referred to "owners of horses" in complimentary terms, but it is the chapandazan and not the khans who appear in the picture. If indeed the khan horse owners were on hand, one can only wonder at their reaction to the Taraki address. "It should," he proclaimed, "have been a matter of great honour for participants to have played skillfully and successfully this ancient game in the era of triumphant '*khalki*' revolution" and "the strong champions are well aware of the Saur Revolution as are all hard working people of the country. The People's Democratic Party of Afghanistan . . . succeeded in wresting power from oppressors and feudal lords."

The speech then pursued a Marxist class analysis across a wide range of issues important to the regime. Most emphatic was the promise of land reform that would strike directly at the traditional khan sponsors of buzkashi. Whatever their true sentiments, the Northern horsemen could only applaud. The newspaper picture shows the very same individuals who a year earlier had clapped for Daoud. One responded to express "their profound backing of their khalqi government and party and . . . their great leader, Noor Mohammed Taraki."[6] Shown for the first time on television and feted at the House of the People, the Kabul buzkashi had fulfilled its elaborate predictions. Dispute-free, it testified to at least some measure of authority. Through no other symbolic event had the new regime been better able to further the impression of its own legitimacy.

That impression, however much bolstered by such efforts as the Kabul buzkashi, soon proved fatally insufficient. Violent resistance spread to every province, and factionalism within the House of the People reached a pitch unprecedented even for Afghanistan. In September 1979, Taraki was murdered and succeeded by his vice-president, the tyrannical and quite possibly insane Hafizullah Amin. Amin lasted only three bloody months before he too was shot, but in that interval a regime virtually bereft of political assets deemed it worthwhile to stage the yearly tournament, now timed "to mark the sixty-second anniversary of the Great October Socialist Revolution."[7] Ominously, this buzkashi was reduced from twelve days to eleven: Bamiyan Province, whose mountains have always obstructed centralization efforts, was by now outside the effective control of Kabul and sent no team.

Late in December Amin died at the hands of his exasperated Russian patrons. Eighty-five thousand Soviet troops installed Babrak Karmal as the new client head of state, but what small semblance of legitimacy had been developed by the two previous regimes was now utterly forfeit. Rebellion turned into war. The winter that followed was most emphatically not one for festive toois, but word of one buzkashi did reach the Western press. In March, 1980, *Newsweek* magazine reported that 50 Russians had been slaughtered at a game in the North.[8] A U.S. diplomatic source later provided details, ultimately unverifiable, but almost certainly true in essence: that the contest in Mazar-i-Sharif had been planned as a trap, that the soldiers had been invited as guests, that they had become engrossed in the game, and that the buzkashi riders had caught them unawares. The same bizarre scenario supposedly repeated itself shortly afterwards in the northern town of Pul-i-Khumri.

Subsequent events showed that, at least in the Afghan context, authority must ultimately be founded on more than coercive force. Whatever fond hopes the Soviet leadership may have had for a peaceful occupation were soon dispelled, and by the summer of 1980 its generals had been given *carte blanche.* Where armored columns failed, helicopter gunships succeeded. The result, however, was not civilian compliance but a combination of death, depopulation, and the refusal to yield. Round-the-clock regime control never extended beyond large towns and main roads. Elsewhere there was no acknowledgement of authority, except when its more massively armed agents happened to be on the spot. Even in downtown Kabul, firefights riddled the nightly curfew, and morning patrols found Russian heads in garbage cans. Much of the populace fled as refugees, but not in acquiescence or resignation. "How can you cut our problems in half?" repeated one displaced khan in Peshawar, Pakistan. "That's easy: give half of us guns."

Coercion, not legitimacy, maintained the Karmal regime, but to what purpose? Except for a handful of officials in Kabul, the situation offered no rewards, and even these men could never count their spoils beyond the next coup. The Soviet politburo, far from elated with an expansionist *fait accompli,* found itself in a quagmire: embarrassed and debilitated. Hence the need for brute force to be accompanied by powerful and familiar symbolic representations in the quest for regime legitimacy. Karmal and his cohorts did as their various predecessors had done and sponsored a national buzkashi tournament.

As usual, the 1980 version was bannered beneath government newspaper mastheads: "Championship Buzkashi games held in Kabul." Karmal did not attend the first day, but in his place the regime vice-president strove for legitimacy:

> Buzkashi is a manifestation of the spirit of the struggle of our people and a shining example of the rich cultural heritage of our country. This year the autumn buzkashi contests begin at a time when the ideals and aspirations of the new evolutionary phase of the Saur Revolution are getting realized one after another. . . . But our enemies, the criminal U.S. imperialism together with the Peking chauvinists, send counter-revolutionary bands, mercenaries, and professional murderers from Pakistan. . . . These traitors and exported bands are treacherously trying to prevent the people from performing their traditional economies and living their normal and humane lives.
>
> These professional thieves and criminals even steal and annihilate the buzkashi horses which are raised and trained with large sums of money and great efforts for the local game."[9]

At the post-tournament reception, Karmal himself made much the same appeal (whose import survives even the awkwardness of Ministry translation):

> The people of Afghanistan are really valorous Muslims. You have preserved your traditions, and your national sports among them the prideful national game of Afghanistan buzkashi, inherited from your fathers and forefathers. This move of yours trembles the enemies of Afghanistan. [10]

The same edition of the Kabul *New Times* (which the *Times* had become) shows Karmal in chapandaz cap and northern cloak which had been presented to him, in addition to six buzkashi horses, by two provincial buzkashi presidents (of Balkh and Baghlan) whom I remember well from my time as powerful men in their localities and vociferous supporters of Daoud. Somehow they had survived the cycle of coup and countercoup, perhaps because of the alternate buzkashi frame: these men could always represent themselves as political simpletons and maintain to successive sets of officials that their participation was "only for fun."

By itself, the 1980 Kabul buzkashi may have been in some ways impressive. It had, after all, been held in conformity with established practice, and in this sense one aspect of the chaotic national experience had been rendered predictable. The traditional essence of buzkashi, furthermore, spoke to heritage. Both predictability of occurrence and traditionalism of genre are the stuff of which legitimacy is symbolically represented.

In relative terms, however, this tournament reflected the weakness of its sponsor. Only seven provinces supplied teams. Now the absentees included not only Bamiyan, but also Takhar and Parwan where Soviet attacks had recently stalled. The buzkashi lasted not twelve days, nor even eleven, but only five. A picture in the *New Times* of December 2 shows spectators clustered in close rectangular groups, while other rows of Ghazi Stadium are completely unoccupied. As a U.S. Embassy cable explains, only card-carrying party members and those for whom they could vouch were admitted. The volatile potential of buzkashi situations had been all too vividly demonstrated the previous winter. This time, the sponsor opted for security rather than expansiveness. It was, in effect, a compromise; better to have a smaller buzkashi than none at all, but better also to be safe than sorry.

That as many as seven teams came from more or less remote provinces does represent considerable sponsorship accomplishment. Several of the best chapandazan in Afghanistan are recognizable from the newspaper photographs, and one can only wonder what sort of coercion went into this display of legitimacy. Earlier in the Olympic year, star members of two national teams had defected and fled into exile rather than represent an illegitimate regime in Moscow. Wrestlers and footballers, these athletes were certainly less provincial, and presumably less intractable, than the buzkashi horsemen, for whom any form of external control is anathema. And one can likewise only wonder what sort of reception awaited the riders on their return home after the fact of collaboration. Only the most intense pressure could have forced them to play. For that matter, only the most securely organized logistics could have transported them safely to Kabul.[11] Towards both these ends, the regime must have taken, and inflicted, great pains. One man's story under such conditions is told in the epilogue.

Not everyone was impressed. A vicarious report on the 1980 tournament from one Afghan refugee now in Germany recalls the tendency of rural khans to discredit the buzkashi toois of their rivals. There were, he had heard from someone who had been in Kabul at the time, "no real chapandazan [clearly an exaggerated disparagement], only some simple people. It was not interesting. Most of the horse owners are in Pakistan now and in the mountains fighting the Russian army, and the most famous people were killed by the Marxist government."

As this book was first written, the Great Game had begun again in earnest. It was "playful," however, only for alien superpowers. The Afghan perspective resembled that of a buzkashi carcass: "Like a goat between two lions," mused Amir Abdur Rahman, who in 1901 was the last khan of Kabul to die of natural causes with his authority still intact."[12] For those whose shouq interest is buzkashi, world reaction to the Russian initiative presented one immediately familiar feature. Who better than the horsemen would understand the principle of Olympic boycott? The first half of 1980 resounded with rhetorical speculation on the link between play and politics. The Moscow tooi came and went. Some guests accepted its invitations, others did not. Level of competition, fairness of adjudication, adequacy of accommodation—all these issues were debated back and forth by rival factions, just as in buzkashi. It is a remarkable irony that the ambiguous relationship between the 1980 Olympics and world politics was perhaps most readily appreciated by back country traditionalists in the very nation whose misfortune prompted the issue.

For the Afghans themselves, even in 2002, authority remains an obsessive problem. With political ties always in flux, individuals rise and fall in lonely arcs. Success is transient; failure trips at its heels. Whole lifetimes are perceived as ephemeral. Their accomplishments—like the conquests of Alexander, Genghiz Khan, the British Raj, the Soviet Union, and Operation Enduring Freedom—recede in time until even the vital names themselves merge in legend and finally disappear. This philosophical perspective has few adherents, however, and does little to ease the compulsive quest for authority. Virtually all men participate in the process; some are briefly successful; but none can hold the political calf forever. It eludes the grasp

HABIB WITH FAMILY MEMBERS IN HIS HOME VALLEY, APRIL 1977. He and his three sons all wear telpaks.

and falls to the ground where another cycle starts. Only the Sufi stands aside, and few share his sense of deviant clarity.

Most men, instead, are like Habib, who, when I last visited him, was well into his 60s. He had been a buzkashi chapandaz for more than half a century and, by his own admission, knew no other way of life—at whatever level of game. One day late in April 1977, we sat on a carpet that his sons had spread by the streambed next to their village, far from town. Spring in northern Afghanistan is as idyllic as it is brief, and this particular afternoon seemed almost magical. For once the stream fairly gurgled, and its valley and even the steppe beyond shimmered in generous green. Both water and color would dwindle within a month, but it was hardly a moment for harsh prospects. Instead we sprawled in a sun too expansively warm for the questionnaire I had prepared. Its structure seemed too much like business, and Habib began to regale me instead with one anecdote after another.

Most dealt, at least at the outset, with his own buzkashi exploits: often heroic, but never really boastful and occasionally quite comic.

Inevitably those stories led into life beyond buzkashi: from the details of his relationship with some horseowner khan to an estimate of the khan himself; from the disruption of a tooi to its political circumstances.

From narrative to narrative, the cast of characters varied with Habib himself as their only common link. For a while he had ridden the horse of such and such a khan, but then had switched to another patron, and then another. He spoke repeatedly of his family, particularly of his father, but otherwise the ties in his life had come and gone. Gradually there emerged from the stories his own sense of social persona: a man inclined towards fellowship but ultimately alone, loyal by nature but forced into opportunism. Above all, he said, he had to be wary. Even at his age, there was no respite from vigilance. It was like that spring day, he said, beautiful and peaceful, but dangerous and certain to change. You could never take it easy, never relax.

The afternoon waned and we both felt an early chill. Habib had kept a quilted winter cloak tucked in a ball behind him, but now he hunched forward and wrapped it across his shoulders. For a lost moment he stared at his fingers, turned them over and back, and then slowly began to trace the bit of intricate carpet between us. Before I left for town, he told one last story.

> It was in the month of Dalw [February] and I was on my way to the tooi of Hajji Latif in Ishkamish. You remember, Whitney, you were there. Two strangers passed me on the way and asked me where I was going. I told them, "To the buzkashi of Hajji Latif."

> Then one of them said, "You must know, *baba* ['old man'], that not far from here lives the famous chapandaz Habib."

> "Habib?" I said, "Habib? I have never heard of this man."

> "Oh, baba," they laughed at me, "How is it that you are so ill-informed? Are you the sort of man who has never been abroad in the world?"

> "This Habib," I asked them, "is he about my age?"

> "Send your children to school, baba, since you are too old yourself," one man said. "Habib is young and vigorous, not an old man like you."

> "How big is he?" I asked.

> "Habib, were he but here with us, would make two or three of you, baba. Habib is a man who could move you over a mountain."

> I thought to myself how times had changed and asked them if their village had a khan whose guest house I could use to pass the night.

> "Hajji Jura Khan has a grand guest house and Habib has stayed there, but you, baba, had better find a place in the mosque where no one will trouble you."

They went their way, and I told them nothing. You remember the buzkashi, Whitney? You remember that one calf I took when the salem was 800 afghanis and Ghafour never even reached it? I did well, did I not? And yet, you know, it is different now. My father died last year. He was 96. Now I am alone with only my own sons. Every year the policeman comes and asks me to play in Kabul. Every year I play. But now I feel old, and my telpak [the chapandaz cap] is loose on my head. My head, I think, has lost some of its meat. I feel old and alone, but what can I do? All my life I have played. How can I stop?

NOTES

[1] Cohen, *Two-Dimensional Man*, p. 8.

[2] Peacock, James, *Rites of Modernization* (Chicago: University of Chicago Press, 1968), p. 241.

[3] Turner, Victor, *Dramas, Fields, and Metaphors* (Ithaca: Cornell University Press, 1967), p. 33.

[4] The *Kabul Times*, October 23, 1978.

[5] The *Kabul Times*, November 5, 1978.

[6] The *Kabul Times*, November 5, 1978.

[7] The *Kabul Times*, November 8, 1979.

[8] The *Kabul Times*, November 8, 1979.

[9] The *Kabul New Times*, December 2, 1980.

[10] The *Kabul New Times*, December 6, 1980.

[11] In the spring of 1980, some eight months earlier, resistance fighters in the North attacked a bus carrying the Afghan national field hockey team back from competition in the Soviet Union. Several players were killed or captured as collaborators. The buzkashi horsemen, who were otherwise honorably known in their northern provinces and whose duress must have been widely understood, would not have faced the same degree of rural antagonism, but their trip to and from the Kabul tournament was bound to have been extremely risky.

[12] Of the fifteen men who have subsequently ruled—or tried to rule—from Kabul, five have been assassinated (Habibullah in 1919, Nadir Shah in 1933, Mohammed Daoud in 1978, Noor Mohammed Taraki in 1979, and Hafizullah Amin in 1979), four were exiled (Amanullah in 1929, Inayatullah after three days in 1929, Mohammed Zahir in 1973, and Babrak Karmal in 1986), one was executed by more or less legitimate authority (Bacha-i-Saqao in 1929) and one was castrated and executed by the Taliban (Najibullah in 1996). Only two relinquished power in reluctant but orderly form (Sibghatullah Mujeddidi in 1992 and Burhanuddin Rabbani in 2001). Not included is a sixteenth, Taliban "Commander of the Faithful" Mullah Mohammed Omar who tried to rule from Kandahar and disappeared in late 2001. Hamid Karzai, the able and well-intended incumbent, sits on a hot seat.

6

FOR REAL (1978–2002)

"Somebody could easily plant a bomb. Let's have more tea."
—Peshawar buzkashi entrepreneur, January 1988

"If you want to know what we're really like, go to a buzkashi game." When this advice was first offered, casually and with no sense of foreboding in 1972, neither the speaker (Afghan diplomat) nor the listener (American counterpart) could have dreamed how disastrously wrong things would go. Apart from one violent interregnum which lasted less than a year (1929), Afghanistan had gradually coalesced—both as concept in mind and a country in fact—for nearly a century. International buffer status kept it low-tech and culturally traditional. The cold war safeguarded its independence and territorial integrity. Soviet influence was paramount but not especially aggressive. All sides got along, watchfully, and there were even moments of humor. U.S. ambassador Robert Neumann was able to quip in a 1973 embassy pep talk, "They're Hertz, but we're Avis. We try harder." We all chuckled.

"Now the real buzkashi has begun." By the time of that remark, late April 1978, I'd lived the game and knew what the speaker (dean of students at Kabul University) meant. Once again, however, neither he nor I could ever have guessed how brutal it would be or how long it would last. A brave and committed man, Dr. Anwar Sultan declined the offer of a U.S. visa extension and hurried home to his family in suddenly transformed Kabul.

Abruptly, all familiar assumptions were up for grabs. In particular, the notion of political legitimacy was now repeatedly challenged. The same Musahiban subset of the Mohammedzai clan had ruled the country for 49 years and, despite internal upheavals, had come to

125

seem an ongoing fact of life. Now a small band of Marxists, to everyone's amazement including their own, suddenly found themselves in power. Their ineptness—Louis Dupree proclaimed Afghan Marxism "more Groucho than Karl"—encouraged both factionalism within their own ranks and the first stirrings of Muslim Resistance. Fragile in the best of times, legitimacy was further jostled and finally shattered by ten years of Soviet invasion, then by various configurations of *mujahedin* (holy warriors), and then by the Taliban.

Power is as power seems. Prior central governments had done all they could to portray themselves as the legitimate repositories of power, including the staging of government buzkashis. All these carefully nurtured impressions collapsed. Most non-kin-based institutions and structures disappeared. Old leaders fled or were killed. In their place arose ambitious, often self-made individuals who, one after another, struggled for control.

Quick-study journalists, new to Afghanistan and in search of cultural hooks, seized on buzkashi and the first edition of this book to explain the bewildering, multisided tug-of-war. And each player—on whichever side—managed impressions in the style of a buzkashi tooi-wala sponsor. Presentation was as important as actual performance, especially in the quest for outside support. The seven designated Resistance parties were themselves clients of more powerful sponsors in Pakistan, America, and Arabia. Each was headed by an individual who curried favor by representing himself and his party as best capable of implementing and sustaining the anti-Soviet effort: in buzkashi terms, of running a tooi. As this chapter is written—late January 2002—no one individual or force has succeeding in taking the *buz* (goat carcass) of power in hand and riding free and clear. Can Hamid Karzai's Interim Authority—backed by the world's most powerful sponsorship—do so? Perhaps.

Despite two dozen years of utter disaster and devastation, the game of buzkashi has itself thrived, albeit in several phases and forms. As chapter 5 describes, the new communist regimes in Kabul at first tried to maintain the October tournament as a demonstration of continuity and control. Despite early Soviet military successes, fewer provincial teams appeared each year in the capital.

Chapter 4 discusses the inevitable tension that simmered in prewar times between traditional rural power elites and the encroaching central government. Old-line khans acquiesced when necessary and, when possible, withdrew into their accustomed *de facto* political autonomy. Such men of local power and prestige were the buzkashi tooi sponsors, horse owners, and chapandaz employers on whom the game depended. For decades, prior to 1978, they had been gradually relegated to the sidelines, both figuratively and literally. Now the crisis in central regime legitimacy and authority enabled these khans to reverse the trend. Culturally as well as politically, the old-line khans were, almost to a man, diametrically opposed to communist rule.

Still, in the early 1980s, word went forth from Kabul: There will be, as in the past, an October capital city buzkashi. Communist provincial governors ordered the khans to field teams. Increasingly, the khans ignored this previously irresistible command. To obey was to support a force that was not only militarily rapacious but also religiously illegitimate. "Go weep," said Idanthrysus the Scythian in response to an unenforceable demand from Darius in 519 BCE. The khans, in effect, began saying the same to Babrak Karmal, whom Soviet power had illegitimately installed on the throne of Kabul. He summoned; no one came. So far as I know, his regime abandoned the Kabul buzkashi tournament effort in 1982.

Thereafter buzkashi and, more broadly, equestrian activity were declared "backwards" by the communist regime and even to some extent proscribed. Various edicts forbade the assembly of horsemen. My buzkashi friends, for the most part cultural traditionalists with long memories, interpreted these prohibitions in historical terms. In consolidating power over Central Asia during the 1920s, the Soviet Union had battled mujahedin frequently mounted, whom they called *basmachi* (bandits). Now the same term was applied.

One ancient Turkman in a 1980s refugee camp outside Peshawar, Pakistan, had been born and raised north of the Oxus River in what is now Uzbekistan. On horseback with sword in hand, he'd ridden against Soviet troops six decades earlier. "Then they went from village to villages killing horses. Afterwards, we hid on foot behind the corners of houses and smashed the infidels with shovels as they passed."

Having fled south once (into Afghanistan), he had now been forced to do so again. "We began as a group from Jowzijan on horseback last year. Many were lost because the infidel pilots shoot at horsemen. They call us basmachis, the same as last time. We are mujahedin, the same as last time."

The nadir of buzkashi inside Afghanistan came at the time of maximum Soviet control, approximately 1983–1986. Buzkashi was still played but only in the most remote hinterland or with the connivance of local Afghan communist authorities. When the tide of war turned, in part because of better-supplied mujahedin and in part because of communist exhaustion, buzkashi revived in the countryside.

The conflict, however, had demanded knowledge and skills usually not possessed by the old-line khans. Power shifted to a new and much younger generation of Resistance "commanders" (*commandan*) who, like their predecessors, were dependent on followers whom they attracted by spoils and the prospect of more spoils. Principally these spoils came in the form of weapons, other war equipment, and (less often) cash either sent from Pakistan or captured from the enemy.

In the same way that potential recruits calculated which would-be leader could supply the best spoils, so these commanders came to Peshawar and shopped from one Resistance party to the next in search of guns and money. Thus equipped, commanders returned to Afghanistan in the hope that their support groups had not dwindled away. As before, images of mastery had to be constantly managed and displayed. As before, buzkashi sponsorship became one format for display and evaluation. To the usual tooi evaluative criteria (number of guests, richness of prizes, pervasiveness of control) may have been added one more. Are the rumors true of Soviet prisoners being used in lieu of the animal carcass? I met one—but only one—commander who, face to face, claimed/admitted having staged such an event. "Ten thousand people were there that day," his nephew later boasted.

Even before the mujahedin capture of Kabul in 1992, buzkashi was being played freely again all across the North. With the country still in turmoil, however, nothing like the old national (ten-province) Kabul tournament was possible. In buzkashi terms, we were back before 1953. There was talk of reviving the tournament, especially among northern factions who now had unprecedented power in Kabul, but "for real" buzkashi—armed conflict against other factions and then against the Taliban—took precedence.

Then, in another abrupt reversal, buzkashi was forbidden again as Taliban Islamist control spread first to Kabul and subsequently north of the Hindu Kush in the late 1990s. Taliban objections to the game echoed what I had heard from some mullahs in mid-1970s Kunduz: That horses should be saved for God's work—often phrased as *jihad* (holy war)—and not wasted in frivolous, ego-oriented pursuits. The Taliban were also overwhelmingly Pushtun, and their occupation of the North amounted to an ethnic as well as a sectarian crusade. Thus Taliban prohibition of buzkashi also had much the same military aim as that of the Soviets earlier: to deprive the non-Pushtun opposition of equestrian capacity.

But while they outlawed kite flying, not even the Taliban could suppress—or resist—buzkashi. In the last winter of their rule, I was approached quite systematically in Peshawar by a well-born and apparently very well-connected young Talib from the movement's spiritual center of Kandahar. His purpose seemed to be back-channel public relations: to explore with a long-ago U.S. official ways to enhance the Taliban image with Americans. As spoils of war in 1998 Maulawi Azizullah had acquired (almost certainly commandeered/stolen) land near the northern city of Mazar-i-Sharif whose *Dasht-i-Shadian* is the Yankee Stadium of buzkashi. He prided himself on two buzkashi horses, doubtless "acquired" the same way, and said that the Taliban, after due consultation with religious authority, had made an exception in their ban on games and were supporting buzkashi "to show the Northern people that we are all brothers." Languid, thin boned, and faintly effeminate with his eye shadow and exquisitely tied turban, Maulawi Azizullah did not play himself: "I have an Uzbek rider to do all that hurly-burly for me. When he wins on one of my horses, all the people up there know who I am."

The players change, but the game, its meanings, and its purposes endure. Nowhere were these unchanging elements more apparent than in the Afghan refugee culture of Peshawar during the 1980s. Originally a Turkic game, buzkashi had been played indigenously only north of the Hindu Kush. Even the Kabul tournament, while welcome fun in the old days, had always seemed to the horsemen a sort of bizarre aberration. Peshawar was even further from home, indeed in another country, and its inhabitants were overwhelmingly Pushtuns, the ethnic nation most disliked and resented by traditional buzkashi folk. Even so, in the winter of 1987–88, I witnessed a sequence of buzkashi events in Peshawar whose day-to-day activity replicated the old patterns with uncanny precision.

Peshawar is situated, in reality as well as romance, at the "settled" end of history's fabled Khyber Pass. Beyond that 24-mile sequence of craggy defiles lies Afghanistan from which, by various routes, more than three million refugees poured into Pakistan during the 1980s. When I first visited—on a nonchalant winter weekend from Kabul in 1972—the population may have totaled a quarter million. By 1987 there were two million Afghan refugees in and around Peshawar. Total population unknown. Things were shifting too fast for a census. It was, in theory, a Pakistani city and Pakistani authority held sway, but one felt the Afghan presence everywhere.

While most Afghan refugees eked out an existence in camps on Peshawar's outskirts, the more enterprising tried their luck in town. Busses and three-wheeled "rickshaws," powered by glorified lawnmower engines and driven increasingly by Afghans, linked the city's three main sectors. Afghan day laborers, antique dealers, and money changers (three quite different populations) clogged the narrow, twisting Old City streets around Qissa-Khawani (Story Tellers) Bazaar. The Cantonment, a relic of British colonial days, was more geometric and less Afghan, but both the hardest manual labor and the most valuable carpets were handled by refugees.

Expatriates (diplomats, humanitarians, media people) lived mostly in a leafy suburb called University Town. They (we) worked hard and played hard—the latter in either the American Club or in a mostly French establishment known as the Bamboo Bar and suspected by Anglo-Saxons as being druggy and decadent. We all had offices during working hours, and the very most enterprising of Afghans came in search of us there.

More than once I recalled F.G. Bailey's *Stratagems and Spoils.* We ex-pats, in effect, represented the spoils: untold wealth in the form of CIA military assistance, refugee relief programs, and exotic academic scholarships. The Afghans concocted stratagems to convince us (this or that ex-pat cornucopia) that our money would be put to best and serious use in certain hands. Proposals appeared on the doorstep and so, occasionally, did carpets. Battlefield tours were available; one Resistance party, the National Islamic Front for the Liberation of Afghanistan run by a Sufi saint and former Peugeot dealer, guaranteed to get journalists back the same day *with* an Afghanistan dateline to show that they'd "been on jihad."

And yet, as even the Taliban were later to realize, no experience quite equaled buzkashi. The fact that Peshawar winters were tropical compared with those of northern Afghanistan—and that horses would overheat as a result—did little to inhibit two entrepreneurs who, realizing the game's singular ex-pat appeal, struggled against each other to control buzkashi presentation. Each, in effect, was an ongoing tooi-wala from week to week. Each hoped that the ambassadors, UN officials, and NGO (nongovernmental organization) directors would come to *his* game and be received as *his* honored guest and go away with a impression of *his* competence to handle volatile situations—all, of course, in the name of friendship and hospitality.

Erving Goffman's "What is it that's going on here?" reverberated in my mind. The ex-pats—or sometimes top Pakistani politicians or generals likewise intrigued by the game—would have a great time, accept sponsor kindnesses (tea and cookies at halftime, carpets for bigwig "chief guests" at game's end), be escorted to their expensive vehicles by the solicitous sponsor, and head home all aglow with exotic experience. What a day!

Then, three or four days later, the sponsor-entrepreneur would present himself at the chief guest's office, express hope that its occupant had had enjoyed himself at the buzkashi, and, seemingly beside the point, just happen to mention such and such an project that would, like buzkashi, be "good for the people" and lacked only the start-up funds.

More than immediate spoils were at stake. Longer-term possibilities loomed. After nearly a decade of suffering under Soviet invasion and (attempted) occupation, Afghanistan seemed poised for some sort of liberation. Ronald Reagan in Washington had given Stingers to the Afghan Resistance by way (ominously) of Pakistan's secret service. Mikhail Gorbachev in Moscow realized better than anyone else how badly, perhaps fatally, the USSR had been bled by Afghanistan. Diplomats were meeting and, on April 14, 1988, would conclude the Geneva Accords committing Soviet forces to leave Afghanistan the next year. Refugees considered return, and men like two khans calculated prospects not only around Peshawar, but also in post-conflict Kabul.

These were serious calculations, made no less so by the fact that their fulfillment has been postponed by another 14 years (thus far).

Calculations continue today. One has to do with who will control sports in newly constituted Afghanistan. Who will be the new president of the Afghan National Olympic Committee? Despite its non-Olympic status, buzkashi is Afghanistan's most notable game. Whoever rules buzkashi is a serious candidate for the ANOC presidency . . . and all its international spoils.

The two rival entrepreneurs in 1987–88, both friends of mine back then, will be known here as Aid Khan and Camp Khan. Both were raised in Baghlan, the province directly south of Kunduz and a crossroads of northern Afghanistan. Both professed to love buzkashi for its own sake and to present it "for the good of the people." Both wooed the ex-pat community with great charm and guile. Despite these similarities, they came from different backgrounds and were equipped with different resources. Those differences are instructive.

Aid Khan was resident director of a German-sponsored and well-endowed NGO, which funneled deutschmarks into Afghan refugee relief. He was, to put it politely, his own accountant and thus had access already to considerable funds. These, he reckoned, could be used to generate more. Aid Khan had two other advantages. First, he had made the pilgrimage to Mecca and thus enjoyed hajji status. Second, as a Mohammedzai Pushtun, he was linked to the erstwhile ruling family. His father, he told me proudly, had once slugged Babrak Karmal (communist president of Afghanistan from 1979–1986) in the National Assembly two decades earlier. Third, like many of the ruling elite, he had learned non-Afghan languages: excellent German and quite good English. Aid Khan's NGO office was itself in University Town, and he maintained another base in a large, long-established, predominately Pushtun refugee camp (Nasserbagh) close by. Aid Khan, in short, was very much at home in ex-pat culture. Like other Muslims, he was barred by Pakistani law from our uniquely alcohol-licensed clubs, but otherwise Aid Khan mixed freely with Peshawar's European and American community.

Camp Khan, whom I knew better, was "commander" of a refugee camp several miles outside Peshawar. Uniquely in Peshawar's environs, this camp catered to northern Afghans already familiar with buzkashi. Culturally and spatially, the residents of this camp were distanced from Pushtun Peshawar. I conducted resident fieldwork there for a few weeks and came to know the logistics firsthand: a shared Suzuki ride downtown, a bus ticket to the University, and another fifteen minutes on foot to my other home in the ex-pat ghetto.

Camp Khan, of course, had his own red Land Cruiser, among the ultimate SUVs in Peshawar, and cruised the streets with driver and armed bodyguard. Even so, he was much less at home in town than Aid Khan. Camp Khan claimed descent from an old Bokhara family. "Bokhara" evokes nostalgia among many northern Afghans: a lost

Golden Age of Central Asian Islam. Land for the camp reportedly had been purchased from a son (or grandson—stories varied) of the last emir of Bokhara. Camp Khan's family had crossed the Oxus River into Afghanistan generations earlier and settled in Baghlan where, depending on whom you believed, they were "prominent land owners and supporters of the people" or, alternatively, "peasants." Whatever his pedigree, he knew buzkashi in his bones and played it as well as a medium physique allowed.

As yet, however, Camp Khan had traveled only once outside the region. He was not yet a hajji. To his great frustration, he knew no European languages and had to depend on translators including myself. Nor did he have an effortless source of funds on the order of those provided to Aid Khan by his German NGO. His money came piecemeal from rents and other charges on refugees in the camp.

Hence the two rivals, while both from Baghlan, represented quite different backgrounds. Aid Khan could call on an array of modern resources: world languages, Western manners, liquid assets, and a base in town. Camp Khan, while very much on the make and anxious to be modern, had basically traditional equipment: northern Afghanistan languages, customs, knowledge, and a camp headquarters well outside the city. Aid Khan was slick, up to speed, and analogous to the government structure that in pre-war Afghanistan had produced rasmi buzkashi. Camp Khan was shrewd, rural, and doggedly irrepressible. His analogue was the old-line khan structure that had staged quami toois.

Each man wanted to be the sole boss of Peshawar buzkashi. Both realized that such status could result in considerable spoils. Their story may seem farcical more than a decade later. At the time, despite the somewhat slapstick skullduggery, it was serious stuff.

Three other characters deserve introduction. The Pakistan government had instituted a Commissionariat for Afghan Refugees (CAR) shortly after the exodus began nearly a decade earlier. One member of this office, known here as CAR Official, was detailed to oversee, regulate, and, if necessary, take charge of Afghan refugee buzkashi. An able man in a cumbersome bureaucracy, CAR Official maintained ties with many people in the buzkashi community and shared tidbits of information with me. CAR Official acted as a kind of mediator/referee between the two ambitious buzkashi khans. They needed his goodwill and courted him accordingly.

The U.S. vice-consul in Peshawar at the time was not only dedicated to his work but also energetically interested in local culture. Several years as a Peace Corps volunteer in pre-revolution Iran had equipped him with excellent Persian, to which he would later add some Pashto. It was he, known here as Vice-Consul, who first put me in touch with Camp Khan. I still value my friendship with this man, now deservedly promoted to much grander things. Each of the two khans recognized his experience and his character but held out hope for the impossible: That Vice-consul would provide some special measure of American largesse.

Inevitably in matters Afghan, I found myself a participant as well as an observer. My formal role that winter was Fulbright professor and scholar, but both khans believed that I possessed personal influence (*waseta*) far beyond that humble status. Both believed that, if treated right, I would use my Persian, my background in buzkashi, and my personal influence—the latter in reality extremely limited—to achieve the great dream goal of bringing buzkashi to the United States.

Enterprising Afghan refugees quickly recognized that the expatriate community there to help them was organized, at least nominally, in terms of institutions rather than individuals. University Town was an alphabet soup beginning with UNHCR (United Nations High Commissioner for Refugees) and extending to the most obscure, even dubious, but always finely titled and acronymic NGO. Thus the Afghans followed suit and sprouted instant organizations complete with logos and letterheads calculated to impress. Aid Khan and Camp Khan were no exception.

Aid Khan had founded the Afghan Mujahedin Sports Association (AMSA) in 1986. He had done so at his own initiative and, he told me poker-faced, at his own personal expense. "It was being played here but in a very disorganized way [by Camp Khan and his associates]. There were games here and there but without true leadership. And the Pakistanis were making it hard, demanding money. Buzkashi needs a real leader who will represent Afghanistan."

In our first interview, Aid Khan spoke of three aims, all "selfless." First, he wanted to save the race—bloodline, or *nasl*—of buzkashi horses. Indeed, it was during his work of organizing horse transport for jihad on behalf of the German-sponsored NGO that he had recognized this need. "These great horses, specially bred for generations, are now in danger because of Soviet attack. So I've told my people in Baghlan to bring their best buzkashi stock here. I have two areas in Nasserbagh: one for stallions, one for mares. They get the best barley, oil, and eggs. God willing, the line will be saved."

Second, Aid Khan wanted to preserve the game itself—"our glorious heritage"—for future generations. "You're an anthropologist. You know how traditions can die out. Look what's happened to Muslim life in the infidel Soviet Union." Third, he aimed to sustain refugee morale. Here Aid Khan echoed every buzkashi sponsor in my 1970s fieldwork experience: "I want the people to enjoy themselves. Jihad is hard. Being a *muhajer* (refugee) is hard. Without morale, we'll lose. With morale—and God's help—we'll free Afghanistan."

Camp Khan had founded the Afghan Mujahedin Olympic Committee (AMOC), intentionally evocative of the pre-war (and hopefully post-war) Afghan National Olympic Committee. Followers already referred to him as "*rais-i-olympic*." On December 18, 1987, Vice-Consul and I were driving to a buzkashi presented and publicized by Aid Khan when Camp Khan rolled alongside—in the full rush of chaotic Peshawar traffic—with his Land Cruiser, driver, and bodyguard. "Where are you going?"

"The Army stadium," Vice-Consul replied. "Isn't there a game today?"

"Oh, that," said Camp Khan. "I don't know. It won't be much. Don't waste your time. The big game is tomorrow. I'm inaugurating my stadium. Hazrat Mujeddidi will be the chief guest. Come then." The red Land Cruiser rolled away.

[I had come to Peshawar to start my work only a week earlier. At this point—chronicling the mid-roadway conversation of December 18—my notes remark: "Well, here it is all over again . . ." 15 years later, I remember exactly the instant of writing those words and the sense that, despite the different country and decade, things between khans were still as they had been in Kunduz long ago.]

We continued to the city's vast and then half-built Army stadium where gathering horsemen competed for field space with adolescent Pakistani cricketers. A few Pakistani police provided the only visible security. Young Afghan men wearing AMSA armbands acted as ushers. Aid Khan presided over a VIP area (called, with typical overstatement, "VVIP section") and awaited the arrival of his chief guest, the Peshawar head of UNHCR. Many other ex-pats were on hand, and more came when the chief guest arrived promptly. He was seated with his family front and center—and next to Aid Khan—on carpets borrowed from local Afghan shops.

This institution of chief guest (*mehman-i-asli*) was new to me. Only in Kabul, where one or another of the royal family used to preside on most days, had there been anything similar in my first study. I soon realized that this status represented the main thrust of what each of the two rival khans was trying to accomplish on any given day. Today Aid Khan hoped to ingratiate himself with the top man at UNHCR. Every well-publicized buzkashi that winter had such a chief guest.

The greater the chief guest, of course, the better. One main hope, all winter long, was to host the American ambassador if and when he came to Peshawar. The ambassador, it was believed, could not only open American coffers but also "in one instant" approve and implement the great envisioned buzkashi extravaganza in the United States. I was an American. I had been a diplomat and was suspected—friendship aside—of still being secretly on the rolls. Both khans would try to enlist me in the ambassador buzkashi effort, each on his own exclusive behalf.

Interestingly, this chief guest feature meant different things to different people. To the ex-pat community on December 18, it was

AID KHAN (white shirt and trousers with dark vest) sits with Pakistani government "chief guest" and family at Army Stadium in Peshawar, January 1988.

UNHCR as a whole—the entire Peshawar institution—that was being hosted and honored; its head was simply the titular representative. Not so for the Afghans and especially for the buzkashi sponsors. Neither Aid Khan nor Camp Khan ever spoke with me of institutions. For them the chief guest was clearly an individual person—like each of them, an individual entrepreneur with whom, hopefully, an individual relationship could be developed.

The buzkashi that day was strictly qarajai, with teams and flags and scoring circles. The score, however, was not kept; nor was there a town crier jorchi to announce scores and praise horse owners. I recognized and spoke with a few horse owners from a decade earlier, but they received no mention. It was more spectacle than competition. Here the riders, the chapandazan, were the main feature. They numbered twenty—two teams of ten each—and their play seemed desultory. My sense of connoisseur criticism was allayed by the on-field presence of Baz Gul, one of the great pre-war riders from Baghlan, who spied me in mid-game and promptly abandoned it in favor of a sideline chat. "Yes, my brother Baz Mir is fine and also your old friend Khair Mohammed. O Whitney, how white your beard has become . . ."

Aid Khan arbitrarily ended the game and presented a carpet to his chief guest with many personal compliments but no mention of

UNHCR. The somewhat bemused recipient then was given turban cloths to present to the chapandazan as their names were called, similar to pre-war Kunduz buzkashis. Baz Gul, who was being given a stipend and a room in Aid Khan's stables at Nasserbagh, maintained a serious and appreciative demeanor but not, he later told me, without some difficulty. "What am I to do with yet another turban?"

The next day—December 19—Vice-Consul and I went to the inauguration of Camp Khan's new stadium next to his camp. Here there were far fewer ex-pats, many more Afghans, and numerous young security guards with Kalashnikovs. The "stadium" consisted of a walled, rectangular enclosure about 200 yards long and 100 meters wide. Cars and pedestrians entered at the far end facing a pavilion similar in concept to that of pre-war Kunduz. We were greeted by Camp Khan, given chairs in the third row, and then were obliged to wait, like everyone else, for chief guest Sibghatullah Mujeddidi, leader of the Afghan National Liberation Front.

The ANLF was one of seven Resistance parties officially recognized by the Pakistan government and thus eligible for jihad assistance of various sorts. Such aid—weapons, medicine, food, or (best of all) cash—came ultimately from government and private sources further afield, mostly in America or Arabia. Pakistan's main intelli-

SIBGHATULLAH MUJEDDIDI, "chief guest" and jihad leader (white beard and turban), arrives at the buzkashi inaugurating Camp Khan's new playing field "stadium" outside Peshawar, December 1987.

gence service, known as ISI, distributed this enormous largesse as it deemed fit. (As the Western public belatedly realized after September 11, 2001, most of this 1980s assistance went to extreme Islamist parties whose ideology prefigured the Taliban.) Mujeddidi's party was well down the list of jihad aid recipients, but even so there were fat pickings. While a Pushtun and a non-northerner, he like Camp Khan was a "moderate," and both supported the cause of ex-king Zahir Shah. Mujeddidi was sometimes called "Hazrat," a Sufi spiritual title held by an uncle executed by the communists in 1979.

Mujeddidi, like other Afghan and Pakistani chief guests, arrived ostentatiously late—in a cavalcade of white jeeps with headlights blazing and horns blaring, precisely an hour after the appointed time. He cut an inaugural ribbon (green for Islam) and spoke to the crowd of how Islam prescribed certain skills, notably riding and shooting, as good practice for jihad. All else being equal, Mujeddidi observed, it was better to be strong than weak.

Thus religiously legitimized, the buzkashi participants appeared in exactly the same formation used at government games in Kunduz and Kabul. Out front rode Camp Khan, in slow solemnity. To my private joy there also appeared the Kunduz jorchi town crier who, once play began, used the old praise chants reworked with jihad emphasis. Even so, as in rasmi games during the 1970s, real communicative power was in the hands of a public address announcer.

Play was much harder than the day before, and a cumulative score was kept. Several hallal/haram disputes arose over whether the carcass was dropped more inside or outside the circle. "Oh chapandazan," called the PA announcer, "Don't quarrel among yourselves. Quarreling among ourselves gets us nowhere." These words, Vice-Consul and I reflected, spoke to central and continuing issues for all Afghanistan.

Shortly after the start, Mujeddidi motioned to Camp Khan and quietly said that the game should last only one hour. Clearly it did not enthrall either this Pushtun chief guest or his grown son who told me that, as an urbanized Kabuli, he had never bothered with buzkashi. Camp Khan hid his disappointment and called the game well before allotted time. Mujeddidi made a short farewell speech about the need for unity, gingerly mounted a closely-held horse for photographs, and departed without further ado for Islamabad.

Even so, as my notes record, purposes had been served. Mujeddidi had been honored by Camp Khan, whose access to ANLF spoils would now hopefully be enhanced. Camp Khan had been publicly honored by Mujeddidi's inaugural presence and had proven himself capable of both building a stadium and filling it. And buzkashi—here I have scrawled "functionalist interpretation" in the margin—had re-intensified both Afghan culture in exile and jihad purpose to regain Afghanistan.

Five days later Aid Khan spoke to me about Camp Khan's stadium inaugural buzkashi. Without my mentioning it, he knew I had been there. "You must have been disappointed. It was staged by one of the political parties. They tried to upstage me and failed. I have no party affiliation. Parties drive us apart. We need bigger men. Mujeddidi made a speech. So what? There were no proper prizes. Not even a proper place to sit in the style of Army stadium. I sent some of my players and some money to be helpful. It was refused. Why do you bother yourself with such people?"

And so it went all winter long. Aid Khan had more money, a more convenient stadium, and a linguistic advantage that let him talk directly with ex-pats like the UNHCR head and Vice-Consul's boss, neither of whom spoke Persian or Pashto. Camp Khan had more authentic roots in the buzkashi community itself and staged more authentic games. In terms of play style and quality, however, there was not much to choose. Each khan had his own core of kept riders. Each tried to lure the other's riders away. All of the games were qarajai with two teams of no more than ten or twelve.

Each khan, interestingly, used the same names for his two teams: Ariana and Bakhtar. These came from ancient, pre-Muslim Afghanistan and were calculated to arouse no partisanship. There had been talk of organizing teams by province of origin or even by party affiliation, but such notions were wisely abandoned as incendiary. Riders told me that the Ariana/Bakhtar identities were meaningless and that they often forgot which was which or even who their teammates were on a given day.

Rivalry was inevitable between the two khans, but this one seemed unusually bitter. Much of the bad feeling stemmed from the previous winter when both men had agreed on a common presentation of buzkashi in Islamabad. They had gone and the game was played, but Aid Khan with his slick talk and urban manners had stolen the show by representing himself to the capital city as buzkashi's sole sponsor.

Camp Khan and his associates were furious. Their anger gave rise to wild accusations. "Everyone knows," one follower told me, "that he [Aid Khan] is a communist, that his German NGO is sponsored by *East* Germany. There's why he has no Resistance party affiliation. No party will have him. He works for the Soviets."

This charge was followed, with wonderful illogic, by another. "He's also getting money from your American Consulate. Do you remember the Army stadium game when your consul, the one who speaks only English, was chief guest? [This game, on New Year's Day 1988, had also attracted Camp Khan and his entourage because of the Consul's importance in Peshawar. Also the consul was recognized as a conduit to the ambassador.] Ever since then, he's been paid by the East Germans *and* the Americans."

Aid Khan made his own political charges. "The reason why he [Camp Khan] has that land in the middle of nowhere [the camp] is that the Pakistan secret service wants to split northern Afghan Resistance forces here in Peshawar and weaken Rabbani [Burhanuddin Rabbani, head of the largely Tajik and "fundamentalist" party Jamiat-i-Islami which ISI did, indeed, oppose]. They gave him the land. He's a Pakistani stooge."

The New Year's Day buzkashi with Peshawar's top American as chief guest refocused minds on attracting the American ambassador. Aid Khan's step-by-step (*qadam ba qadam* in Persian) strategy seemed to work. Clearly the U.S. consul, who later took issue with my suspicions regarding Aid Khan's integrity, had been impressed. Clearly word had been passed to the embassy in Islamabad. On January 5 I learned that Ambassador Arnold Raphel was planning to attend a buzkashi given in his honor by Aid Khan at Army stadium on January 8.

In camp for other research, I ran into Camp Khan the same day and told him the news. He questioned me closely and then said, "Yes, I knew about it yesterday. Too bad, but buzkashi is only a game. It doesn't matter." Had he known about it "yesterday"? Had he known about it at all before I told him? In any case, he hid whatever worry and resorted to the old dismissal, always used when sponsorship runs into trouble, that buzkashi, far from being political, "is only a game."

I was still in camp the next day (January 6) and, over breakfast tea with some elders, mentioned the now settled plans for Aid Khan's ambassadorial buzkashi two days hence. Complete surprise and deep dismay. Camp Khan had not told them the bad news. And it was, they assured me, very bad news indeed. "Now our Camp Khan will lose contact with the Americans," they said. "No contact, no contracts. No buzkashi trip to America. Please, Whitney, can't you do something?"

"No," I said accurately, "There's nothing I can do. It's settled. The ambassador will be chief guest at Aid Khan's buzkashi."

Camp Khan strolled into the room, looking unconcerned. Over tea he denied all sense of disappointment or defeat. Again he said, "It's only a game." Pause and second cup of tea. Then: "They'll be fine. My only concern is safety. Army stadium is such a big place. Someone could easily plant a bomb." Then: "Let's have more tea."

I went back to Peshawar to prepare for the big day. The next morning, January 7—24 hours before the ambassador was due to arrive—Vice-Consul phoned me. "The Pakistanis have cancelled tomorrow's buzkashi for the ambassador. Security problems. There's been a bomb threat."

It was at this point that the government of Pakistan's Commission for Afghan Refugees took a hand . . . or tried to. Cancellation had embarrassed Aid Khan and discomfited the Americans, but it had deeply shamed the Pakistan government. Their officials were, after all, responsible for the whole country and what happened in it. Like any buzkashi sponsor, they tried their utmost to control not only events but also the impressions of events. Image management had been an ongoing problem for the Pakistanis. Bombings and killings were frequent around Peshawar. Most of these were confined to marginal communities, such as the Afghan refugees, and thus constituted only local news. Now, however, Pakistan's weakness was displayed on a larger stage. The government could not guarantee protection for the accredited ambassador of its most valued and powerful ally, the United States of America. President Zia ul-Haq himself was said to be mortified.

CAR Official was put on the case. He called a meeting for January 9 in the dingy, frigid, cavernous concrete structure that housed the Commission. Aid Khan and Camp Khan were summoned—together with a third khan who, sensing chaos, had begun laying groundwork for his own buzkashis—and told that henceforth all buzkashi games, each and every one, would require specific government authorization in advance. All chief guest invitations would likewise be issued by the commission. CAR Official, under orders and not without some private trepidation, thus imposed himself as overall Peshawar tooi-wala. He had already been facilitating security for some games; now he would seek to control all games. He began by banning buzkashi for the forthcoming weekend.

In the Old City I bumped into Camp Khan's younger brother and one of the Resistance commanders who also played buzkashi. There was much talk in the bazaar about an imminent Soviet withdrawal from Afghanistan. "No," said the commander, normally famous for his anti-Soviet zeal, "They can't leave too quickly. The whole world would laugh at them. It would be proof of their incompetence. Like the ambassador's buzkashi that was cancelled. Look at the Pakistanis. And look at [Aid Khan]. He looks ridiculous. Now everyone laughs."

Camp Khan, irrepressible as ever, was in fine spirits when he phoned that evening. It was the first time we had spoken since both Aid Khan's fiasco (which he may have caused) and the CAR meeting (which was supposed to lay down the law). Clearly he did not feel chastened. "What a pity the ambassador could not come to Peshawar. Please tell him that we at this camp can give him a game whenever he desires. He will be safe with us. Don't bother the people at CAR. Deal directly with the ambassador."

The ambassador never came, but not for want of trying on all sides including my own. Instead, and under partially effective CAR surveillance, buzkashis resumed both in the Army stadium and at the camp. Aid Khan seemed to get the better of it. On one day he sponsored a morning game for the German ambassador and an afternoon session for a Canadian contingent.

Anthropologists are supposed to be neutral, but both I and (very privately) CAR Official found ourselves rooting for Camp Khan. Perhaps it was because, between two rogues, he was the underdog. Or perhaps because he was, whatever his faults, a deep-dyed buzkashi supporter. Or perhaps because of what I was told by others about the two men. Both were reportedly involved in what the West calls graft and corruption. Compared to his rival, however, Camp Khan was a mere amateur.

As such, when the time came to please *my* patron, I steered the opportunity towards Camp Khan. My patron was head of "public affairs"—culture and media relations—at the U.S. embassy in Islamabad. He supervised the supervisor of my Fulbright scholarship and had kindly hosted me in the capital city. He called to ask how he and his family could see a buzkashi. That night I called Camp Khan, and a date was proposed. Next day I called CAR Official, and the date was confirmed. Here was "participant-observation" at its most participatory.

The public affairs officer was only number three in our embassy hierarchy, but Camp Khan soon inflated the position to "like an ambassador." Further, he proposed that other Western ex-pats—"as many as possible"—be invited. Special invitation cards were printed, and two days before the game we toured University Town in the red Land Cruiser, complete with AK-47 bodyguard, delivering the notices. "Why not deliver them earlier?" I had asked.

"Don't you remember your time in Kunduz?" Camp Khan replied. "Invite people too soon, and too much can go wrong."

As such on February 11, only two days before the event, a scant handful had any notion that it would take place. That afternoon Camp Khan went into action, not only making the ex-pat rounds with me but also alerting the horse owners, riders and jorchi town criers. (Habibullah, the Jugi town crier from Kunduz, had himself become a sort of entrepreneur by training his brother-in-law and cousin in this specialized role. "When the world learns about buzkashi," he told me, "we'll be ready." Meanwhile they would appear in various combinations at various games. On February 13, all three were there.) Extra folding chairs were rented so that all ex-pats could sit with the VVIPs. Chicken, lamb, raisins, carrots, and mounds of rice were purchased (the makings of a celebratory *pilau*) along with fruit, cookies, tubs of yogurt, and crates of soft drinks—all for the lunch at Camp Khan guesthouse, the equivalent of an old-style tooi-khana.

Much of ex-pat Peshawar arrived in our own SUV convoy about 2 P.M. The U.S. embassy chief guest sat "bala" for lunch, flanked by some friends from Islamabad on one side and one of the numerous Mujeddidis and me on the other. Afghan men sat along one side wall and tried, with commendable decorum, not to look at the ex-pat women sitting opposite.

Both lunch and game went without a hitch. The ex-pats had been counseled to bring the equivalent of shenak, which helped defray expenses. At game's end Camp Khan's chief guest (my patron) awarded 500 rupees (then nearly $20) to each of the chapandazan. Camp Khan walked us to the chief guest's car (which I, my notes read, "as chief guest's follower should have collected and driven onto the field to save him the trouble of walking to it and to underscore his importance). Camp Khan expressed to the chief guest "a world of thanks for your noble presence," and mumbled to me that now was the moment for buzkashi in the United States. He phoned the next day. He dropped by the day after that. And the day after that.

Buzkashi has never been to the United States, but one evening in March it got as far as the American Cultural Center then located at 17 Chinar Road in University Town, Peshawar. In the previous three weeks I had tried—and failed—to bring the rival groups together, in a neutral stadium, for a buzkashi in honor of U.S. Ambassador Raphel. With the help of CAR Official and the advice of Vice-Consul, I'd come close and, in the process, learned a great deal of what confronts a prospective buzkashi sponsor, a tooi-wala. Perhaps I'd come too close to learning too much. One dark interpretation of our failure was that "the Pakistanis don't want these Afghans united." Whatever the reason and after much work on his part as well as mine, CAR Official called and said simply, "Cancelled. The Home Secretary has decided that it's a security risk."

Thus we—the American Center director and I—hit on the idea of an end-of-season soiree. My patron and his family came again from Islamabad, but this gathering had about 150 chief guests: horse owners, young and old chapandazan, all three town criers . . . as well as Aid Khan and Camp Khan and their sizeable entourages. Here was the traditional elite of northern Afghanistan, and—we all naively supposed—they'd soon be going home. What better way to win hearts and minds than by bringing them all together for one last great meal? What better way to spend less than $500 of U.S. taxpayer money?

Invitation cards were issued to guests the day before and required upon their arrival. Weapons were collected, checked, and stacked at the door. Men like Baz Gul (whose waist, it is said, "is as big as a mountain") can eat a lot, and they did: enormous platters of pilau and entire bunches of fruit. After dinner there were speeches, effusive perhaps but sincere. We all sensed a great chance for Afghanistan. We all had great hopes. Then I showed about fifty slides taken up North in the 1970s before the horror had started.

Slide shows are synonymous with tedium in the West. The Center director and I had debated the wisdom of this after-dinner gambit, not least because belching is considered acceptable and snoring could soon follow. But never has a slide show producer been more surprised.

At first there was utter silence. Then murmurs and chatter and even some guffaws as earlier versions of audience members came on the screen. Then silence again and, when I held one picture too long, a scatter of muffled sobs. It was Tosh Mohammed, the great chapandaz from Balkh Province, who had become *shaheed* (martyred) the first year of the war. The same happened when Khosh Mohammed of Kunduz appeared, collecting a salem from the town crier, a then dark-bearded Habibullah jorchi. Khosh Mohammed had tried to stop a tank. That buzkashi had been for real.

Absent from the party but still alive at his home above Khanabad was another Habibullah: the chapandaz Habib who, more than any other, had been my mentor during fieldwork a decade earlier. Several slides were of him. Leaving the Center at evening's end, one Kunduz player said, "God willing, I'll see Habib this summer. I'll tell him that you remember."

Epilogue

HABIB

Life can be more complicated that you think.
—Afghan Refugee, Baluchistan, Summer 1982

"How can I stop?"

Habib's parting question in April 1977 seemed at the time merely personal. All too soon it came to represent, at least in my own mind, the horrific spiral of violence into which Afghanistan fell and kept on falling. This epilogue is meant as a tribute to both Habib and his country.

We never met again after 1977, but word was passed in both directions between the legendary chapandaz and the new anthropologist. His subsequent story deserves telling for two reasons. First, because Habib's story is also that of Afghanistan over the past 24 horrific years. What he encountered and endured is tragically typical. Second, because Habib was always more than typical, was always a hero to people in his valley and his province . . . and was, in a departure from scholarship, a special person to me as well.

Telling his story properly requires one anecdote from the storyteller's own life. Without realizing it at the time, I'd encountered the great Habib years earlier in a Washington, D.C., movie theatre.

Before ever going to Afghanistan, my wife and I and another couple were provided with six months of Dari language training. Our instructor came from the northern Afghan city of Mazar-i-Sharif and delighted in sneaking regional tidbits into our practice dialogues. Lesson 21 contained what for me would be a fateful sentence: "That horse is the best for buzkashi."

I took special, anticipatory pleasure in Lesson 21. True, I was going overseas as a sober government bureaucrat, but nothing could

145

block the sheer exoticism of Afghanistan. And buzkashi, our teacher assured us, was the culture's most vivid event. One day someone mentioned a new film called *The Horsemen.*

Columbia Pictures had gambled: a full-length feature film set in Afghanistan, based on the superb novel by French author Joseph Kessel, and scripted completely without Western characters. It revolved, like Kessel's book, around buzkashi. The father and son protagonists, each a champion chapandaz, were played by Jack Palance, whose famous cheekbones made him look appropriately Central Asian, and the darkly handsome Omar Sharif. Leigh Taylor-Young was later described (Los Angeles *Times*) as "the most beautiful nomad ever born." Otherwise the cast consisted of extras: Afghans in the early shooting and then, when the Afghanistan production phase ended (as planned or in discord, depending on whose account you believe), Spaniards dressed as Afghans on a lot outside Madrid. Eight of the chapandaz buzkashi riders were also taken to Spain for the final six weeks. Given this hodge-podge of personnel and logistics—not to mention the lack of Western characters with whom an audience could identify—it's little wonder that Columbia's gamble failed. Reviews were mixed at best, and *The Horsemen* was a box-office flop.

Our class saw *The Horsemen* together and reveled in it; I went back twice more. The best part comes near the beginning when Omar Sharif and other great riders from all across the North are summoned to the very first king's birthday buzkashi in Kabul. For 420 magnificent seconds, the spectacle of buzkashi itself is front and center.

Usually triumphant in cinema, Omar Sharif loses this time. He grabs the carcass, heads for a score, but then is attacked at full gallop by a grizzled Mongol-looking rider of greater power and cunning. Horses collide, and whips draw blood. The fierce Mongol wrestles the carcass away. Omar falls and is dragged with one foot in the stirrup. The rest of the film, like Kessel's book, deals with his quest for redemption.

We never see the Mongol rider again, at least not up close, and his name is not listed in the credits. Even so, whenever we reviewed Lesson 21, I'd think of the game and see his face and say to myself, "*There's* the Afghanistan I'd like to know. I want to meet *that guy.*"

The meeting was deferred by half a decade. Two years of embassy work and then three years of graduate study passed before I started buzkashi research in the northern provinces. My initial host and guide was the government appointed "president" of Kunduz buzkashi. On the first Friday afternoon in December 1976, he introduced me to "his" Kunduz team. One of them was *that guy.* His name, I learned, was Habib.

Habib wasn't the biggest and, I suppose, no longer the strongest. It had been seven years since the *Horsemen* shoot, and by now he was in his 60s. "*Shast shikast*," they say in Afghanistan: "When you're 60, you're broken." Habib wasn't broken yet, but, as I came to realize, he played like an old gunslinger who'd lost his fast draw: picking his spots and keeping his back to the sun. None of these subtleties registered on me at the moment. I was blown away by the Hazara (Mongol-descended) cheekbones, the leathery skin, and the enormous hand that shook mine, ever so gently.

I settled in: to the village, to the language, to field anthropology, and—as winter set in—to buzkashi. My host made me part of his traveling entourage, a dozen men who went with him from buzkashi to buzkashi. All winter long we ranged—often on horseback—across the latitudinal band of provinces that constitute northern Afghanistan. Even when the khan and I took his Russian jeep, it was just to get close. Once near the game, we'd greet his retainers who'd gone ahead, swing onto our waiting horses, and arrive in massed equestrian splendor. This togetherness was always phrased as "friendship," but I tingled at the knowledge that we were also the khan's support group, a private army in case "for play" became "for real."

Habib played in most games. Usually he'd conserve energy and then surge at a special moment—the akherulaq last round of play, for instance, when the day's top prize money was offered. Sometimes, when the action was slow and poorly rewarded, he'd rein his horse next to mine and provide expert commentary: How some riders were good at getting the carcass off the ground (zamin-gir), others at snatching it from someone else at full gallop (chakka-gir). How riders who were friendly—or whose khan horse-owners were friendly—would run interference for each other or whip each other's horses on the rump. How cheats would hide a length of rope up their sleeve (*chelburse*) and use it, for a fleeting instant, in order to secure the carcass beneath one leg (*takom*).

Play would last into late afternoon, and then we'd all retire to the guesthouse of this or that notable for an evening of dinner and stories. One frequent cycle of narrative has already been described in chapter 1, the Turkman folk hero Kurroglou, who rises to leadership and power by a combination of charisma, shrewdness, and personal bravery. Exploit leads to exploit as ever more supporters flock to his banner. Life is briefly glorious, but treachery lies in wait and Kurroglou dies by the knives of assassins. This story from the seventeenth century still describes the essential dynamics of Afghan politics.

Then as now, the horse is romanticized as more trustworthy than humans. The more human loyalties become compromised, the more a hero like Kurroglou must come to depend on his mount. His horse, unlike his associates, never lets him down. Kurroglou's greatest feats are always accomplished with the help of his legendary stallion, Kyrat.

It is Kyrat who enables his master to run down villains, save noble damsels, and make hairbreadth getaways. As long as his horse is present, Kurroglou remains invulnerable. His eventual killers must kill the horse first. They slash the veins in all four of Kyrat's legs. Only then does Kurroglou, the heroic horseman, acknowledge final defeat.

This epic comes from the same cultural tradition as buzkashi. Until quite recently the entire Eurasian steppe from the Black Sea to the Wall of China was dominated by people who lived on horseback. It was a world in flux: physically nomadic, fluid in its social ties, volatile with the potential for sudden conflict. Livestock, the essence of survival, were constantly liable to loss from disease or marauders. Allies were equally problematic. Political ties shifted with the momentum of events. Leaders rose and fell. A khan was recognized as a khan only so long as he could dominate the political field, score impressive victories, and provide his supporters with spoils. In my fieldwork era the dependence on horses had mostly disappeared, but buzkashi remained as the ritualized enactment of this tradition. Its horseowner khans still tried to impress the public and attract supporters. And its embodied heroes were the great riders, the chapandazan, like Habib.

Other evening guesthouse stories dealt with more recent events. Like all pre-mass-media peoples, Afghans are skilled narrators, and here Habib, because of his cinematic excursion to Europe, was in frequent demand. His audience was not so well traveled. Some listeners had not been even to Kabul; only the few pilgrims to Mecca had been further. Static-plagued transistor radios were beginning to provide BBC and VOA—and Radio Moscow in flawless Persian—but Habib was the real deal: not only a horseman hero but also an authority on the wider world. He'd been in person to the Land of the Franks.

One evening I taped stories from that fabulous adventure: Habib at a bullfight (which he found unmanly), at a fancy restaurant (where the clinking of glasses together as a toast seemed to him like the Afghan game of knocking hard-boiled eggs together until the weaker breaks), lost at night on city streets (and amazed because the police were helpful rather than abusive "despite my being a Hazara and from another qaum").

There were more stories on that last April afternoon in Habib's village. He showed me a bundle of gun catalogues that he'd gotten in Europe. Typical of Afghan men, Habib loved guns. We spoke of buzkashis and toois rumored for the next season. It was when we spoke of the future that sadness crept into his face. As a young man, I could barely begin to understand. And then his final question: "How can I stop?"

Dusk fell. I went back to town and then back to America. Afghanistan fell apart in the spring of 1978. And time would prove that Habib could not stop even when he tried.

For several years I had little word from Kunduz and almost none about Habib. A Marxist coup had toppled legitimate rule. The Soviet Union had invaded, tried to occupy the country, and now was destroying it instead. Then, in the blisteringly hot summer of 1982, I found myself with Afghan refugees in Quetta, Pakistan.

Already the refugees were everywhere. Most had settled in make-shift camps of canvas tents, mud walls, and reed mats. Late one August afternoon, my driver and I trudged around one of these shan-tytowns. Its inhabitants clustered disconsolately in what shade they could find. One clump of faces blended into the next. Then suddenly a man stared at me, as if somehow in this ragged stupefaction there existed a glint of meaning between us. "Aren't you Whitney?"

It took a moment, but I remembered. We had met several times during my field research up north in the mid-1970s. He'd been a person of modest substance, not a khan by any means but someone whose life was firmly established. Now he had only a dirty tent with its scraps of carpet, charred pots, confused wife, and sick children.

It was an embarrassed reunion—awkward for us both because he now had so little and I, as if by miracle, had been transformed from fieldworker (i.e., alien incompetent) to established academic. We fled to reminiscence, the stuff of better times. Did I remember such and such a person, place, event? Such and such a horse and buzkashi? I'd left Kunduz more than four years earlier; he'd escaped only six months ago. There was a lot to tell. And eventually, of course, we got to Habib. I started my tape recorder. Afghans, even in exile, were still great storytellers.

"Most of your buzkashi friends are scattered now: some martyred, others in prison, others in the mountains, others only God knows. Some have probably collaborated with the Communists. Life can be more complicated than you think, Whitney. But Habib—I can tell you about Habib, at least until the time I myself left Kunduz half a year ago. After that, I don't know. Only God knows.

"He's not what he was, you know. He's old now. But even so everybody still knows him because of buzkashi. Habib rode the horses of other men, the khans, but even so he himself acquired a name. 'Habib chapandaz, Habib chapandaz,' they would say in the bazaar when he passed. And the police, of course, know where he lives up the valley from Khanabad. They used to send for him to play in Kabul before the king. Now there's no king, but they still know.

"So the regime, the Parchamis [the communist faction then in power] wanted to use his prestige. They got him from the village and made him go to the Hazarajat [a mountainous area in central Afghan-istan] where most of his qaum still live. They made him say that he was against the Resistance. I don't know much about it, but when he came back home the Resistance people around Khanabad were really furious with him. They didn't shoot him or cut his throat. He was Habib, and as boys they had all heard his name and watched him play and tried to be like him. In those days there was no one as strong as Habib. Now he's old, and the men understood how the Parchamis had put pressure on him, but even so they were furious.

"So they told him he had to stay at home. He couldn't go to the bazaar. They wouldn't let him. For five, six, seven months he couldn't go to the bazaar in Khanabad. His sons could go but not Habib. It's a shameful thing, you know, to be shut up that way. For all that time nobody saw Habib in the bazaar.

"Then he started to help the Resistance in secret: give them food, you know, and even let them borrow his horse, the good one he had in your time. And then his brother's son, Kareem, was becoming a Resistance leader. He led one raid when they captured 170 Kalashnikovs. Not bad. 170! So they finally let Habib go to the bazaar. But now the Parchami spies would be after him so he never stayed long in the bazaar, and never went far—only as far as the produce market (*mandawi*) on the outskirts of town.

"One day it happened. They were on their way back from town, on their way up the valley. Oh, there must have been fifteen or twenty horsemen. It had been bazaar day, Monday. They were on their way back about noon when the plane attacked. Why? I can't tell you why. The Russians think everyone on horseback must be in the Resistance. They remember that much from the time of their wars against Bokhara [late nineteenth century with uprisings into the early 1930s]. And it's true. To be in the Holy War, you need but two things: a horse and a rifle.

"One bullet struck the horse on top of its head and came out its neck. The horse was hit ['ate bullets'] in all four legs. All four! Habib, thanks to God, wasn't hurt at all. I don't know why not. Only God knows.

"The horse kept going. It didn't fall. Five bullets and it didn't fall. It took Habib as far as some trees, where he hid until the plane went away. Some of the other people also made it; some didn't. Habib got down, and then the horse lay down and went to sleep. It wasn't dead, only sleeping. And when the plane was gone, Habib woke the horse and got back on. The horse delivered him all the way home. The whole way! Only then did it die ['surrender its body to God']. It was Habib's own horse, the one you yourself remember.

"Now I don't know. Before I left Khanabad, they fired that BM-16 up the valley. The new rockets. They make water boil and walls disappear. And now it's been seven months—two in Kunduz, one on the way, and four more in this camp—so I can't tell you any more about Habib. I don't know. Only God knows."

I sent my driver ahead and walked back the hour and a half to Quetta. This unlovely city, rebuilt by the British after a 1935 earthquake, is a dusty oasis rimmed with craggy, unforgiving mountains.

Now the sun fell behind them, and within minutes the western sky-line went from fuzzy, blinding dazzle to coal black silhouette. My feet scuffed and shuffled in the dust, not wanting to get anywhere. Still in my early 40s, I suddenly felt old and remembered what Habib had said, that last day, about how his chapandaz cap, his telpak, was loose because his head had "lost some of its meat."

Then I remembered the epic of Kurroglou and his faithful wonder horse Kyrat. The parallels with Habib's story were unmistakable: human treachery, equine fidelity, even the wounds in all four of both the horses' legs. Habib, unlike Kurroglou, had escaped, but only to suffer the further agonies of Afghanistan.

In that years that followed, other Kunduz refugees came to Pakistan. Some—including the fine Pushtun chapandaz Ahmad Gul and his Turkman rival Zol—were old friends from my mid-1970s study. Habib never came. He remained, I was told, "safe at home" in the hills above Khanabad. Yes, he still played sometimes or at least rode on the outskirts of buzkashis. No, the "atheist Russians" and their "country-selling" Afghan henchmen no longer bothered him. Yes, Ahmad Gul and Zol would give him my regards. Years passed. Ahmad Gul was martyred; Zol has lost some teeth but still plays hard. I went back to other parts of Afghanistan and yet, because ethnically mixed Kunduz province remained a treacherous free-fire zone, never to Habib's valley.

The instabilities were seismic as well as political. In February 1998 an earthquake struck Takhar province, next to Kunduz, and an English friend went to report for the BBC. He sat-phoned me e-mails about local buzkashis, now flourishing again in the post-communist era and undeterred by the recent natural disaster. I asked him to ask about Habib.

The reply came back: "Your friend Habib died quietly three years ago. Everyone remembers him as a great player and hero. By the way, his nephew is now a top player. This new man remembers how his uncle spoke of you. He sends regards."

I went to the bookshelf and opened *Horsemen of Afghanistan*, the magnificent photographic study of buzkashi by Roland and Sabrina Michaud. Habib occupies page 34, standing in his stirrups. You see the top of the saddle horn. Above it are Habib's massive hands tightening the red sash (*cammarband*) that fails to keep a brown corduroy cloak in place across his chest. His right hand holds the buzkashi whip (*camcheen*). Habib's shoulders are flaired, and his Mongol face, mouth open and eyes wide, is fully alive. The telpak sits on his head.

"But now I feel old," he had said that last day in 1977, "and my telpak is loose on my head. My head, I think, has lost some of its meat."

Not in this picture. The telpak fits fine. There's nothing loose about it. Habib is saddled up and set to play.

Glossary

Akherulaq final round of tudabarai play in any given session, typically rewarded with the session's biggest prize

Amir recognized leader of Muslim forces, especially in pre-nation-state polities

Arbab government appointed village headman

Baba grandfather, old man

Bacha-i-kaka patrilateral first cousin

Bala "high" and honored seating position within a group

Basmachi native "bandit" enemies of Soviet control in Central Asia and later Afghanistan

Buz "goat" carcass in buzkashi, even when a calf is used

Buzkashi goat grabbing or goat dragging

Chakka-gir buzkashi technique of snatching the animal carcass from another rider

Chelburse cheating technique in which a cord, hidden up one's sleeve, is used to secure the animal carcass to the saddle horn

Chapandaz specialist buzkashi rider (pl. chapandazan)

Commandan Anti-Soviet Resistance commander

Dehqan farmer, peasant

E'tibar personal credit, dependability, trustworthiness

E'tifaq cooperation

Hajji honorific title recognizing accomplishment of the pilgrimage (hajj) to Mecca

Hallal permitted by Islam, also used in qarajai buzkashi to describe a carcass dropped inside the scoring circle

Haram forbidden by Islam, also used in qarajai buzkashi to describe a carcass dropped outside the scoring circle

Hisiyat personal character

Jihad   Muslim holy war

Jorchi   town crier, in buzkashi the mounted announcer of prize money and praise chants

Jur personi   greeting, "asking after health"

Khalq   faction of the People's Democratic Party of Afghanistan, which first came to power after the leftist coup of April 1978

Khan   traditional honorific informally bestowed in recognition of power and importance

Khesh   noncorporate (ego-centered) group of relatives by marriage (affines) with whom a buzkashi sponsor claims identity and on whom he depends for support

Ma'awen   deputy; second in provincial buzkashi structure to the rais-i-buzkashi (pl. ma'aweneen)

Majles   council, meeting

Mehman-i-asli   "chief guest" of refugee buzkashis in Pakistan

Mehmandar   host (lit. one who has guests)

Mirab   locally appointed organizer of irrigation systems

Muhajer   refugee (pl. muhajerin)

Mujahed   holy warrior, one who performs jihad (pl. mujahedin)

Mullah   Muslim cleric

Mustufy   second ranking civilian in provincial government bureaucracy

Nam   prominence, reputation, "name"

Nasl   race, bloodline, genetic strain

Oghlaq   Turkic term for buzkashi, also transliterated as *ulaq*

Parchami   faction of the People's Democratic Party of Afghanistan, which came to power with the Soviet invasion of December 1979

Payan   "low" and unexceptional seating position within a group

Pilau   a rice-based dish with lamb, carrots, and raisins

Qadam   step (as in qadam ba qadam: gradually, progressively, or "step by step")

Qarajai   the newer, mostly government-inspired form of buzkashi with fixed spatial goals including flags and circles

Qaum   flexible but fundamental unit of group identity, usually ethnic and patrilineal (agnatic) and therefore corporate, but sometimes used to denote regional or occupational groupings

Qaumi   belonging to traditional social structure, "tribal"

Rais-i-buzkashi   government appointed "president" of provincial buzkashi structures and teams

Rais-i-olympic   "president" of the pre-war Afghan National Olympic Committee

Ramazan   Muslim lunar month of fasting, known in Arab countries as Ramadan

Rasmi   related to government, "official"

Rish Safed   elder, "white beard"

Salem prize announced during buzkashi play and presented to winning rider

Sawarkar horseman; noncompetitive rider on outskirts of buzkashi competition (pl. sawarkaran)

Serai traditional, rectangular building surrounding spacious open patio and used for commerce and/or accommodation of travelers and livestock

Shaheed martyr in the cause of Islam

Shenak voluntary but expected contribution given to buzkashi sponsor by guests upon arrival and used to help defray sponsorship expenses

Shouq special and individual interest, passion, or pastime (such as buzkashi)

Sufi Islamic mystic

Taqom technique of securing the animal carcass by swinging one leg over it and pinning it against one's horse

Telpak fur-fringed lambskin cap worn by recognized chapandazan

Tooi celebration, traditionally of circumcision or (less frequently) marriage, providing occasion for buzkashi; more narrowly, the rite of passage itself

Tooi-bashi closest collaborator of buzkashi sponsor and general on-field manager of tooi buzkashi

Tooi-khana main tooi headquarters where guests are initially received

Tooi-wala sponsor of tooi and buzkashi

Tudabarai older, more traditional form of buzkashi in which the aim is to ride with the carcass free and clear of all other players

Waseta personal influence

Waqf income-earning religious trust

Zamin-gir buzkashi technique of snatching the animal carcass from the ground

Index